INNER HEALING MINISTER'S MANUAL

A PRACTICAL GUIDE FOR SOUL HEALING
AND WHOLENESS IN CHRIST

INNER HEALING MINISTER'S MANUAL

A PRACTICAL GUIDE FOR SOUL HEALING AND WHOLENESS IN CHRIST

TOM CORNELL

SOZO PUBLISHING

CONTENTS

INTRODUCTION
CALLED TO HEAL THE BROKENHEARTED

When Jesus stood up in the synagogue in Nazareth and read from the scroll of Isaiah, He declared His mission:

"The Spirit of the Lord is upon Me, because He has anointed Me to preach the gospel to the poor; He has sent Me to heal the brokenhearted, to proclaim liberty to the captives and recovery of sight to the blind, to set at liberty those who are oppressed; to proclaim the acceptable year of the Lord." (Luke 4:18–19 NKJV)

This passage is more than just a historical moment. It is a declaration of the Kingdom mandate. The same Spirit that anointed Jesus now rests upon His body, the church. We are called to continue His ministry—to proclaim good news, to break chains, to open blind eyes, and yes, to heal the brokenhearted. Isaiah 61:1 NKJV says it this way:

"The Spirit of the Lord God is upon Me, because the Lord has anointed Me to preach good tidings to the poor; He has sent Me to

heal the brokenhearted, to proclaim liberty to the captives, and the
opening of the prison to those who are bound."

Notice the language: heal the brokenhearted. That's not just metaphorical. It's real. It's practical. It's needed. Jesus knew that the human soul—the seat of our mind, will, and emotions—carries wounds that only His presence can heal. And He didn't just come to save our spirits for eternity. He came to restore our souls in this life.

This manual is about stepping into that part of His ministry. It is about equipping you as a minister of inner healing, so you can partner with Jesus in bringing His comfort, restoration, and wholeness to the broken places in people's lives.

Inner Healing and Deliverance: Two Sides of One Coin

Too often the church has separated deliverance and inner healing as though they were competing ministries. Some focus only on casting out demons, while others focus only on counseling wounds. The truth is, they are inseparable.

Deliverance addresses the enemy's presence and influence. Inner healing addresses the wounds and lies that gave him access in the first place. If you cast out demons but leave the wound unhealed, the enemy often finds his way back in. If you try to counsel wounds without dealing with the spiritual oppression attached to them, the person often feels stuck.

Freedom requires both. Inner healing and deliverance are not two different gospels—they are two expressions of the same gospel of the Kingdom. Jesus cast out demons, yes. But He also sat with the broken, restored their dignity, and rewrote their stories with His truth.

This is why I am releasing this Inner Healing Minister's Manual alongside the Deliverance Minister's Manual. They belong together. They complement one another. If you want to be fully equipped, you need to understand both.

Why Inner Healing Matters

The world is full of people walking around with invisible wounds. Abuse, neglect, betrayal, abandonment, rejection, trauma, and sin all leave scars. These wounds shape the way people think, feel, and live. They become the root system of destructive patterns—addictions, anxiety, anger, fear, perfectionism, and relational dysfunction.

Left unhealed, wounds distort identity. A person may know the truth in their head, but their heart still believes lies: "I'm unworthy. I'm unlovable. I'll always be rejected. God can't really love me." These lies don't just sit dormant. They attract darkness. Wounds become open doors for the enemy to gain influence.

This is why inner healing is central to Kingdom ministry. It's not optional. If we want to see disciples truly transformed, if we want to raise up sons and daughters who walk in wholeness, we must learn to minister healing to the soul.

Jesus didn't just cast out demons. He restored the woman caught in adultery. He touched the leper who felt untouchable. He healed Peter's shame after denying Him. He went after the Samaritan woman's thirst for love and gave her living water. He didn't just break chains—He bound up hearts. That's the model we follow.

The Minister's Posture

Before we dive into the process, I want to talk about posture. Inner healing is not a technique—it's a posture of the heart. This ministry requires compassion, humility, submission, and dependence on the Spirit.

Compassion

If you don't love people, you shouldn't minister inner healing. This is not about proving your authority, building your reputation, or checking boxes. It's about loving people enough to sit with their pain, to weep with those who weep, and to patiently walk with them until Jesus touches the wound.

Compassion says: "I see you. I hear you. I value you." When someone feels safe and loved, they are able to open the locked doors of their soul. Compassion disarms fear. It creates an atmosphere where Jesus Himself can enter.

Humility

Inner healing ministers must stay low. We are not the healer—Jesus is. We don't have all the answers. We don't "fix" people. We simply create space for the Healer to show up.

Humility also means we don't pressure people. We don't force memories. We don't push them faster than they are ready to go. We honor the person's pace and the Spirit's timing. Healing that is rushed often retraumatizes. Healing that flows from humility restores.

Submission

We are under authority. Inner healing ministry is not a solo project. It must be practiced in alignment with the local church, under covering, and with accountability. Lone rangers get into trouble. Submission keeps us safe.

Submission also means submitting to the Spirit. We don't run a script. We follow His lead. Sometimes He goes straight to forgiveness. Sometimes He sits in silence. Sometimes He surfaces a memory we never expected. Our job is to follow, not to control.

Spirit-Dependence

This ministry only works because the Holy Spirit shows up. You cannot heal trauma by human wisdom alone. You cannot break lies by positive thinking. You cannot integrate fragments by pep talk. It is His presence that heals.

Every session begins and ends with dependence: "Holy Spirit, we need You. Jesus, come and do what only You can do." If He doesn't show up, nothing happens. But when He does, everything changes.

The Culture of Safety

Before people will let you into their deepest wounds, they need to feel safe. Many who need inner healing have lived in unsafe environments. Abuse, betrayal, and rejection have taught them that people can't be trusted. If you don't carry safety, their protectors will shut the door.

Safety means you carry yourself with integrity and purity. You are beyond reproach. You don't minister alone with the opposite gender. You have a helper present. You keep confidentiality. You respect boundaries.

Safety also means you don't pressure people. You only walk with them as far as they are ready to go. If Jesus doesn't push them, neither should you. You simply open the door, invite Him in, and let Him do the work.

This culture of safety is part of the Kingdom. It's how Jesus ministered. He never manipulated. He never coerced. He always invited. And that's how we minister too.

What This Manual Is and Is Not

This manual is not meant to replace professional counseling or medical care. There are situations where trauma is so severe that professional help is necessary, and we should not be afraid to refer. We honor the work of counselors, therapists, and doctors.

What this manual does is equip you, as a minister of the gospel, to partner with the Spirit in bringing Jesus into the wounded places of the soul. It gives you practical tools, language, and structure to walk people through the process of healing.

This is not a quick fix. It's not a magic formula. It's a journey. But it is a journey Jesus loves to take with His children. And you get to be a guide along the way.

The Flow of the Manual

Here's how we'll walk together:

- Part I lays the foundation—what inner wounds are, what the Bible says, and the posture of the minister.

- Part II walks you through the process—how to prepare, identify wounds, present Jesus in the pain, lead forgiveness, break vows, heal fragments, address soul ties, and deal with deep traumas like ritual abuse.
- Part III gives you tools—Scriptures, prayer, prophetic ministry, worship, dreams, and even understanding the body-soul connection.
- Part IV focuses on aftercare—helping people rebuild identity, walk in community, establish boundaries, and sustain freedom through spiritual disciplines.
- The appendices give you practical resources— prayers, session guides, forms, quick-reference cards, and Scriptures.

By the end, you'll not just understand inner healing—you'll be equipped to minister it.

A Final Word Before We Begin

If you are reading this, it's because God has called you. He is raising up deliverers in our day, just like in the book of Judges. Not superheroes, but sons and daughters filled with His Spirit, carrying His compassion, and walking in His authority.

You don't need to be perfect to do this. But you do need to be willing. Willing to sit with pain. Willing to love without agenda. Willing to follow the Spirit. Willing to give Jesus all the glory.

My prayer is that as you walk through this manual, you will not only learn how to heal the brokenhearted—you will become one who carries healing everywhere you go. That you will see Jesus show up in memories, in wounds, in tears, and in whispers of truth. And that through you, the captives will be set free, the broken will be made whole, and the Kingdom of God will come on earth as it is in heaven. Let's begin.

PART I

FOUNDATIONS OF
INNER HEALING

1

THE NATURE OF INNER WOUNDS

EVERY PERSON YOU WILL EVER MINISTER TO HAS ONE THING IN common: they carry wounds in their soul. Some wounds are obvious, others are hidden. Some are fresh, others have festered for decades. Some come from traumatic events, others from subtle patterns of neglect or rejection. But in every case, the wound is real, and it shapes the way a person thinks, feels, and lives.

Before we talk about how to bring healing, we need to understand the nature of these wounds—where they come from, how they manifest, and why Jesus alone can heal them.

Trauma, Abuse, Loss, and Sin

The soul—the seat of the mind, will, and emotions—can be wounded in many ways. Trauma is one of the most common. Trauma happens when an event overwhelms a person's ability to cope. It leaves them feeling powerless, terrified, or trapped. Abuse is another major source. Physical, emotional, verbal, or sexual abuse all cut deeply into the soul. Loss is another wound-maker: the death of a loved one, the loss of innocence, the collapse of a marriage, the betrayal of a friend. Even sin wounds the soul—not only when people sin against us, but when we sin against others or ourselves.

These experiences do more than hurt in the moment. They get stored in the soul as pain, fear, shame, anger, or despair. The person learns to survive, but often at a cost. They build walls, make inner vows, or develop coping strategies. But the wound remains.

When someone is wounded, it affects every part of their being. It distorts how they see themselves, how they relate to others, and how they view God. A woman abused by her father may find it hard to trust men—or even to see God as a loving Father. A child abandoned by their parents may grow up believing, "I am not worth staying for." These wounds don't just create pain; they create lies that shape identity.

Wounds of Sexual Abuse

Few wounds cut deeper than sexual abuse. Because sexuality touches the deepest parts of our identity, when it is violated, the impact is profound. Sexual abuse leaves people feeling dirty, ashamed, and powerless. It often leads to confusion about identity, difficulty forming healthy relationships, and cycles of secrecy or addiction.

As ministers, we must approach this area with extreme caution and compassion. Survivors of sexual abuse are often hyper-vigilant—they can sense if you are safe or unsafe within minutes. If they do not feel safe, they will shut down. That's why your posture matters so much. You must carry tenderness, patience, and purity.

When ministering to someone with sexual abuse wounds, remember these cautions:

- Do not rush. Healing takes time. Forcing memories can retraumatize.
- Do not probe. Let the Holy Spirit surface what needs to be healed. Don't ask graphic questions.
- Do not shame. Many survivors already feel it was somehow their fault. Make it clear it was not.
- Do not isolate. Always minister with accountability, especially in cross-gender situations.

The healing journey for sexual abuse often involves helping the person invite Jesus into the memory of the abuse, letting Him speak truth into the lies, and walking through forgiveness —not excusing the abuser, but releasing the debt to God. Sometimes it involves breaking soul ties, renouncing shame, and reclaiming identity. But at every step, the survivor must feel safe, honored, and empowered.

Sexual abuse wounds can take years to heal fully. That's okay. You are not responsible for finishing the work in one session. Your role is to create an encounter with Jesus that moves the person one step closer to wholeness. He is the faithful Healer who will complete what He begins.

Signs of Inner Wounds

How do you know when someone is carrying inner wounds? Sometimes they tell you directly. More often, the wounds show up indirectly through patterns of behavior, emotions, or relationships. Here are some common signs:

- Emotional triggers. Small events cause disproportionate reactions—anger, fear, tears, or withdrawal. These reactions are tied to unhealed memories.
- Self-sabotage. People undermine their own success, relationships, or spiritual growth because they subconsciously believe they don't deserve good things.
- Destructive cycles. Addictions, broken relationships, perfectionism, or chronic anxiety often point to deeper wounds.
- Hyper-vigilance. People always on guard, unable to rest or trust.
- Shame and self-hatred. An internal voice that says, "I'm bad. I'll never be enough."
- Spiritual blockages. Difficulty receiving God's love, hearing His voice, or trusting His Word.

These symptoms are not the real problem—they are the fruit of unhealed wounds. If you only address the symptoms, you'll never see lasting change. But if you go to the root—the wound itself—and invite Jesus into that place, the fruit will change.

Think of it like a tree. If the roots are poisoned, the fruit will be too. You don't heal the tree by painting the fruit. You heal the tree by purifying the roots. Inner healing goes to the roots.

Spirit, Soul, and Body Dynamics

One of the most important things to understand in this ministry is how the spirit, soul, and body interact. Scripture makes it clear that we are three-part beings. Paul prays in 1 Thessalonians 5:23,

"Now may the God of peace Himself sanctify you completely; and may your whole spirit, soul, and body be preserved blameless at the coming of our Lord Jesus Christ."

The spirit is the part of us that connects to God. When we are born again, our spirit is made alive in Christ. The soul is the seat of our mind, will, and emotions. The body is our physical frame. These three parts are distinct but deeply interconnected.

When the soul is wounded, it affects the body. Trauma often manifests as physical symptoms: chronic pain, stomach issues, autoimmune flare-ups, or even unexplained illnesses. Likewise, when the soul is wounded, it can hinder the spirit's expression. People may struggle to hear God, trust Him, or walk in faith—not because their spirit isn't alive, but because their soul is blocking the flow.

That's why healing the soul is so critical. When the soul is healed, the body often follows, and the spirit flows freely. I've seen people delivered of physical pain the moment Jesus healed a soul wound. I've seen people who couldn't hear God's voice suddenly hear Him clearly once shame was broken off. The soul is not a side issue—it is central.

Jesus Heals the Soul

The good news is that Jesus heals the soul. Psalm 23 says, "He restores my soul." That's not poetic fluff—it's a promise. Jesus restores what was broken. He binds up the wounds. He rewrites the lies. He integrates the fragments. He brings peace where there was torment.

The model we teach at SOZO is simple but profound: present Jesus in the memory. When the person is in the wound, experiencing the emotions and lies, we invite Jesus to come. We ask what He is doing, what He is saying, how He wants to heal. And He always shows up.

This is not psychological manipulation. This is not guided imagination. This is encounter. It is the living Jesus stepping into the very place where the wound occurred and redeeming it. When He comes, shame lifts. Lies break. Pain releases. And the soul begins to heal.

The Invitation

As we move forward in this manual, I want you to carry this foundational truth: every person has wounds, and Jesus loves to heal them. You don't need to be intimidated by trauma. You don't need to feel unqualified. If you can carry compassion, humility, and dependence on the Spirit, Jesus will use you.

You will learn how to recognize wounds, how to invite Jesus into them, how to lead people through forgiveness, how to break vows and lies, how to integrate fragments, how to deal with deep traumas like ritual abuse, and how to walk people into long-term wholeness.

But it all starts here—with understanding the nature of inner wounds. They are real. They are deep. But they are not beyond His reach.

Jesus came to heal the brokenhearted. And He has anointed you to join Him in that mission.

Reflection Questions

1. WHERE HAVE WOUNDS SHAPED MY IDENTITY? REFLECT ON the statement: *"These wounds don't just create pain; they create lies that shape identity."* What beliefs about yourself, God, or others might actually be rooted in unhealed wounds rather than truth? What experiences—trauma, loss, rejection, or even your own sin—may have planted these lies? How have these beliefs influenced the way you relate, trust, or receive love?

2. HOW HAVE MY COPING MECHANISMS PROTECTED ME—AND Limited Me? The chapter describes inner vows, walls, hyper-vigilance, perfectionism, and self-sabotage as signs of deeper wounds. Which of these patterns, if any, show up in your life? In what ways have these coping strategies helped you survive? In what ways are they now hindering your spiritual growth, your relationships, or your ability to receive God's love freely? What might it look like to invite Jesus into the root instead of managing the fruit?

3. HOW HAVE I EXPERIENCED—OR RESISTED—JESUS' HEALING in My Soul? Psalm 23 says, *"He restores my soul."* The SOZO model invites Jesus directly into memories and wounds. When you consider Jesus stepping into your most painful experiences, what emotions rise to the surface—hope, fear, resistance, or longing? What wound or memory do you sense the Holy Spirit highlighting as an area He desires to begin restoring? What step of courage, surrender, or openness is Jesus inviting you to take so He can begin healing that place?

2

BIBLICAL BASIS FOR INNER HEALING

BEFORE WE DIVE INTO THE PRACTICES AND PROCESSES OF INNER healing, we need to root this ministry in the Word of God. Inner healing is not a modern invention. It is not psychology with Christian language added. It is the continuation of the ministry of Jesus, empowered by the Spirit, founded in the Scriptures, and practiced by the early church.

If we are going to walk with confidence as ministers of inner healing, we need to know beyond doubt that this is God's idea. When we understand the biblical basis, we will not be swayed by criticism, fear, or unbelief. We will know that when we step into a broken heart and invite Jesus to heal, we are walking in His mandate.

God Heals the Brokenhearted

Psalm 147:3 says it simply and powerfully:

"He heals the brokenhearted and binds up their wounds."

This is not symbolic poetry. This is the nature of God. He is a healer—not only of bodies, but of hearts. When the soul is shattered, God bends down to bind it up. When the heart is bleeding, He applies His comfort. When the emotions are torn apart, He restores.

Throughout the Old Testament, God is revealed as a healer. Exodus 15:26 says, "I am the Lord who heals you." That Hebrew word for heal—rapha—doesn't just apply to physical sickness. It's the same word used when God heals the land, restores a nation, or brings peace. His healing is holistic. It covers spirit, soul, and body.

When David cried out in Psalm 34:18 ESV, *"The Lord is near to the brokenhearted and saves the crushed in spirit,"* he was declaring the same truth: God draws close to the wounded soul. He doesn't despise weakness. He doesn't shame pain. He comes near.

The entire storyline of Scripture is about a God who takes broken people and restores them. From the exile of Israel to the exile of Adam and Eve, God's heart has always been to restore what sin and trauma have broken.

Jesus' Restorative Ministry

When Jesus began His public ministry, He chose Isaiah 61 as His mission statement:

"The Spirit of the Lord is upon Me, because He has anointed Me to preach good tidings to the poor; He has sent Me to heal the brokenhearted, to proclaim liberty to the captives and the opening of the prison to those who are bound." (Isaiah 61:1)

In Luke 4:18–19, Jesus quotes this passage and applies it to Himself:

"The Spirit of the Lord is upon Me, because He has anointed Me to preach the gospel to the poor; He has sent Me to heal the brokenhearted..."

This was not filler. This was not a nice introduction. This was His assignment. Healing the brokenhearted was central to His mission.

And we see Him live it out. He didn't just preach truth. He restored dignity to the woman caught in adultery (John 8). He drew out the deep thirst of the Samaritan woman at the well and offered her living water (John 4). He healed Peter's shame after denying Him three times (John 21). He comforted the grieving sisters, Mary and Martha, and raised their brother Lazarus from the dead (John 11).

Everywhere He went, He healed—not just bodies, but souls. He touched lepers who were untouchable. He welcomed children who were ignored. He spoke peace to storms of fear. He stopped for the desperate. He restored people's stories.

And when He commissioned His disciples, He gave them the same assignment. Matthew 10:8 records His words:

"Heal the sick, cleanse the lepers, raise the dead, cast out demons. Freely you have received, freely give."

Notice He didn't separate deliverance, physical healing, and inner healing. It was all one package. He sent them to bring the wholeness of the Kingdom wherever they went.

How the Early Church Ministered Wholeness

The ministry of inner healing didn't end with Jesus. The early church carried it forward. In Acts 9, when Saul encountered Jesus on the road to Damascus, he was not only delivered from blindness in his eyes—he was healed from blindness in his soul. His hatred, violence, and deception were confronted by Jesus, and he was restored into his true calling as Paul, apostle to the Gentiles.

In Acts 8, Philip ministered in Samaria, and it says,

"unclean spirits, crying out with a loud voice, came out of many who were possessed; and many who were paralyzed and lame were healed. And there was great joy in that city." (Acts 8:7–8).

That "great joy" was not just physical healing. It was the fruit of restored souls.

The letters of Paul are filled with language of inner healing. In 2 Corinthians 10:4–5, he writes about pulling down strongholds and taking thoughts captive. In Ephesians 4:22–24, he teaches about putting off the old self, being renewed in the spirit of the mind, and putting on the new self. In Romans 12:2, he calls us to be transformed by the renewing of our minds. These are all descriptions of inner healing.

James 5:16 says, "Confess your trespasses to one another, and pray for one another, that you may be healed." This is more than physical healing—it's healing of the heart and soul through confession, forgiveness, and prayer.

The early church understood that salvation was not just about going to heaven when you die. It was about experiencing wholeness now. The Greek word sozo, often translated "saved," also means healed, delivered, and made whole. That's why we at SOZO emphasize presenting Jesus in the place of pain. Because the early church carried a sozo gospel—one that heals the whole person.

Theological Foundations for Healing Memories and Identity

One of the most common objections to inner healing ministry is, "Where do you see this in the Bible?" Some people think helping someone revisit a memory with Jesus sounds like psychology, not Scripture. But let's look at the foundations.

God Redeems Memories

In Scripture, God consistently brings His people back to their memories, not to retraumatize them, but to heal them. Over and over, He tells Israel to remember: remember Egypt, remember the Red Sea, remember His covenant. Memory is central to faith.

But memories can also be places of bondage. A traumatic memory can replay like a prison. That's why Jesus must step into those memories—not to erase them, but to redeem them. When He enters a memory, He changes the way it is experienced. The event is still part of the person's history, but the wound no longer defines them.

David models this in the Psalms. He constantly brings his pain before God—his fear, shame, anger, and despair. And every time, God meets him there with truth, comfort, and hope. That's inner healing: bringing the wound into God's presence and letting Him transform it.

God Heals Identity

At its core, inner healing is about restoring identity. Sin and trauma distort who we are. Lies take root. Shame covers us. But Jesus came to restore us to our true identity as sons and daughters of God.

Think of Gideon. In Judges 6, he hid in fear, believing he was the least of the least. But when the angel of the Lord appeared, He called him a mighty man of valor. God redefined Gideon's identity, not based on his wound or his fear, but on God's truth. That is inner healing.

Think of Peter. After denying Jesus three times, Peter was crushed with shame. But in John 21, Jesus restored him by asking three times, "Do you love Me?" and then recommissioning him: "Feed My sheep." Jesus healed the wound of shame and restored Peter's identity as a shepherd.

That's the theological foundation: Jesus heals memories, rewrites lies, and restores identity.

Inner Healing as Kingdom Ministry

Inner healing is not optional or secondary. It is central to the gospel of the Kingdom. When Jesus taught us to pray, "Your kingdom come, Your will be done on earth as it is in heaven," He was inviting us to bring heaven's wholeness into earth's brokenness. There is no trauma in heaven. No shame, no abuse, no fragmentation. When we minister inner healing, we bring the reality of heaven into wounded hearts.

This is why the enemy fights this ministry so fiercely. He knows that when people are healed in their souls, they walk in freedom, authority, and intimacy with God. They no longer believe his lies. They no longer live bound by fear or shame. They step into their calling as sons and daughters who carry the Kingdom.

That's why this manual matters. It's not about theory. It's about equipping you to continue the ministry of Jesus, to heal the brokenhearted, and to restore the wounded places of identity.

Standing on the Word

As we move forward, never forget: inner healing is biblical. It is rooted in God's heart, revealed in Jesus' ministry, practiced by the early church, and theologically grounded in God's plan to restore memories and identity.

When you invite Jesus into a wound, you are not doing psychology. You are obeying Isaiah 61 and Luke 4. You are fulfilling the gospel of sozo. You are partnering with the Spirit to heal the brokenhearted and set the captives free.

Stand on that truth. Let it give you boldness. Let it silence the critics. Let it anchor you when you feel uncertain. You are walking in the ministry of Jesus. And that means you can expect His Spirit to show up every time.

Reflection Questions

1. HOW DOES THE BIBLICAL FOUNDATION FOR INNER HEALING reshape my understanding of Jesus' ministry—and my own calling? Reflect on Isaiah 61, Luke 4, and Psalm 147:3. Before reading this chapter, did you see inner healing as central or secondary to the gospel? In what ways does seeing Jesus as the Healer of memories, identities, and broken hearts expand your understanding of His mission? How does this revelation influence your confidence to minister healing in the lives of others?

2. WHERE HAVE I PERSONALLY EXPERIENCED—OR RESISTED— God's healing in my memories or identity? This chapter shows that God redeems memories, rewrites lies, and restores identity. What memories from your past still influence how you see yourself, others, or God? Are there moments where you sense the Holy Spirit inviting Jesus into a wound—but you feel hesitation, fear, or avoidance? How might recognizing God's nearness to the broken-hearted (Psalm 34:18) change the way you approach those places?

3. WHAT BELIEFS OR QUESTIONS DO I STILL CARRY ABOUT INNER healing—and how does Scripture speak to them? Some people fear that inner healing is "psychological" or unbiblical until they truly see its scriptural foundations. What hesitations, concerns, or misconceptions have you held about inner healing? Which Scriptures in this chapter most challenged or strengthened your perspective? How does understanding the early church's practice of wholeness (Acts, James 5, Romans 12, Ephesians 4) clarify the legitimacy of this ministry today?

3

THE ROLE OF THE INNER HEALING MINISTER

INNER HEALING IS NOT JUST ABOUT WHAT YOU DO IN A MINISTRY session. It's about who you are as a minister. You can have all the tools, prayers, and processes in the world, but if your heart posture isn't right, if your life doesn't carry integrity, if your presence doesn't create safety, the fruit will be limited.

This chapter is about the role of the minister. Not the techniques you use, but the life you live. What kind of person do you need to be in order to partner with Jesus in healing the brokenhearted? What posture do you carry when you sit with someone in their deepest pain? What safeguards keep you healthy, safe, and accountable as you do this ministry?

Servanthood

At the core, inner healing ministry is an act of servanthood. Jesus modeled this when He washed His disciples' feet. He didn't come to be served but to serve (Mark 10:45). That same posture must define us.

Servanthood means remembering: it's not about me. It's not about my gifting, my reputation, or my success rate. It's about the person in front of me. It's about honoring their story, their dignity, and their pace. It's about creating space for Jesus to show up.

When you come into a session as a servant, you posture yourself to listen more than you speak. You don't come in with a plan to fix them. You come in ready to partner with what God is doing. Servants don't control—they serve. Servants don't demand—they provide. Servants don't push their agenda—they yield to the Master's will.

Compassion

Compassion is the heartbeat of this ministry. Without it, you will end up cold, mechanical, or even harsh. Compassion is what allows you to sit in the mess of someone's pain without trying to rush them out of it. Compassion is what enables you to hold back tears as they share their trauma, to be fully present without judgment.

Jesus was moved with compassion again and again. He wept with Mary and Martha at Lazarus' tomb. He stopped for the blind man crying out on the roadside. He touched the leper no one else would touch. Compassion is not pity. It's not just feeling bad for someone. It's entering into their suffering with the love of God and believing for their restoration.

When people feel your compassion, they sense the heart of the Father. And that is what opens the door for healing.

Confidentiality

One of the quickest ways to destroy trust is to break confidentiality. People are entrusting you with their deepest wounds —things they may never have told anyone else. If they share those things and later hear them repeated outside the session, the damage is devastating.

As a minister, you must commit to confidentiality. What is shared in the session stays in the session, except in cases where safety is at risk (such as abuse that must be reported). You don't share details with your friends, your spouse, or your church. You don't use someone's story as a sermon illustration without permission. You guard their trust as if it were treasure.

Confidentiality communicates respect. It tells the person, "You are safe here. I will not exploit your pain. I will protect your story." And that safety is essential for healing.

Covering, Accountability, and Healthy Boundaries

Inner healing ministry is not something you do on your own. You need covering and accountability. Covering means you are submitted to spiritual authority. You are part of a local church. You are not a lone ranger.

When you operate under covering, you have protection. If something goes wrong in a session, you have leaders to stand with you. If you're unsure about something, you have people to seek counsel from. Covering is not control—it is safety.

Accountability means you invite others to speak into your life. You give them permission to ask hard questions about your purity, your motives, and your practices. You don't hide. You walk in the light.

Healthy boundaries are part of this. You know your limits. You don't minister in ways that compromise your integrity. You don't minister alone with someone of the opposite gender. You don't keep secrets that put you in vulnerable positions. You guard yourself and the people you minister to.

Boundaries also mean you know when to say no. You are not the Savior. You can't fix everyone. Some people need more than you can give. Some need professional counseling or medical care. Saying no doesn't mean you failed—it means you are wise enough to know your lane.

Ministers Must Receive Healing Themselves First

One of the greatest dangers in this ministry is when wounded people try to minister out of their unhealed pain. If you have not walked through inner healing yourself, if you have not faced your own wounds, you will project them onto others. You may try to control their process, avoid certain topics, or carry unhealthy attachments.

That's why I don't train my disciples to minister inner healing in their first year. First, they go through the process themselves. They receive healing. They face their pain. They encounter Jesus in their own wounds. Only after that season do I begin equipping them to minister to others.

Even the disciples weren't sent out until Matthew 10. Jesus ministered to them first. He healed their broken places. Then He said, "Freely you have received, freely give." You can only give what you've received. If you try to give healing you haven't received, it will ring hollow.

So let me say it plainly: if you want to minister inner healing, let God heal you first. Stay in that process. Keep bringing your wounds to Him. Stay tender. Stay dependent.

Apprenticeship: Starting as Helper Before Leading

Another principle I emphasize is apprenticeship. Too often people get a little knowledge and rush into leading sessions. That's not safe—for them or for the person receiving ministry.

It is far better to begin as a helper. Sit in on sessions. Watch how experienced ministers listen, pray, and respond. Observe how they handle difficult moments. Learn the flow.

As a helper, you play a vital role. You are praying, discerning, supporting, and sometimes even helping the person process. You are not passive—you are learning actively.

After a season of helping, when your leaders discern you are ready, you can begin to lead. But even then, do so with humility, knowing you are still learning. Apprenticeship protects the ministry, and it protects you.

The Culture of Safety in the Kingdom

One of the most important things you can carry into inner healing is the culture of safety. Without safety, people will not open their wounds. They may come to a session, but their protectors will stay on high alert, guarding them from vulnerability.

Safety is not just about what you say—it's about how you carry yourself. Do people feel at peace around you? Do they sense they can trust you? Do they know you will honor their pace and their story?

Creating a culture of safety means you carry the heart of the Father. He is gentle. He does not break bruised reeds or quench smoldering wicks (Isaiah 42:3). He nurtures, protects, and restores. When people feel that in you, they will feel safe to open up.

Carrying Yourself in a Way That Makes People Feel Safe

Practical safety begins with your demeanor. Speak gently. Listen attentively. Don't interrupt. Don't minimize their pain with clichés like, "Just get over it." Look them in the eye with kindness, not suspicion.

Safety also comes through consistency. Show up on time. Keep your word. Respect boundaries. Follow through. These simple actions build trust.

Remember, many people have lived in unsafe environments. They've been betrayed, abused, or abandoned. They've learned not to trust. So when you carry safety, you are breaking that pattern. You are showing them a new way.

Beyond Reproach: Witnesses, Gender Considerations, Integrity

Part of creating safety is being beyond reproach. That means you avoid even the appearance of impropriety. You minister with witnesses present. If you are ministering to someone of the opposite gender, you make sure another trusted person is in the room.

You also walk in integrity. You don't flirt, manipulate, or use your position for personal gain. You guard your own purity. You honor the people you minister to as image-bearers of God, not as projects or conquests.

Being beyond reproach doesn't just protect you—it protects the person you're ministering to. It creates a safe environment where healing can happen without fear.

No Pressure: Never Forcing Someone Beyond What They're Ready For

This is a critical principle: never pressure people. Inner healing is not about forcing memories, emotions, or breakthroughs. It's about following the Spirit and honoring the person's readiness.

Sometimes people are not ready to face a memory. That's okay. Forcing them can retraumatize. Sometimes they are only ready to forgive partway. That's okay too. Celebrate the step they did take.

The Spirit is gentle. Jesus never forced Himself on anyone. He invited, He asked, He waited. That's how we minister too. We create the opportunity. We ask if they are willing. We honor their yes, and we respect their no.

When people know they won't be pressured, they feel safe. And when they feel safe, they often go further than they expected—because the Spirit leads them at the right pace.

Ministers Who Carry the Kingdom

At the end of the day, the role of the inner healing minister is not about titles or techniques. It's about carrying the Kingdom. Servanthood, compassion, confidentiality, covering, boundaries, apprenticeship, safety, integrity, and gentleness—these are the marks of a Kingdom minister.

If you live these out, you will create environments where people feel safe to open their wounds. And when they open their wounds, Jesus will heal them.

Remember: you are not the healer. You are the servant of the Healer. Your job is to create space, carry safety, and invite Him in. If you do that faithfully, you will see broken hearts restored, lies broken, wounds healed, and lives transformed.

Reflection Questions

1. WHAT PARTS OF MY LIFE, CHARACTER, OR POSTURE NEED TO BE reshaped in order for people to feel safe, honored, and seen when I minister to them? Which of these qualities comes naturally to you, and which ones do you struggle to embody consistently? Do people around you—family, friends, or those you serve—experience you as safe, present, gentle, and trustworthy? What traits, habits, or attitudes is the Holy Spirit inviting you to refine so that the atmosphere you carry more fully reflects Jesus?

2. AM I MINISTERING FROM A PLACE OF ONGOING PERSONAL healing, accountability, and healthy boundaries—or from my own unprocessed pain? In what areas do you still need Jesus to heal you before you try to lead others into healing? Do you have spiritual covering, mentors, or accountability structures speaking into your life regularly? Which boundaries (emotional, relational, or gender-related) do you need to strengthen so that your ministry remains beyond reproach and aligned with integrity?

3. HOW WELL DO I REFLECT THE GENTLENESS AND PACE OF JESUS —never forcing, never pushing, always honoring the person and the Spirit? When someone isn't ready to go deeper, how do you usually respond—internally and outwardly? What would it look like for you to model the gentleness of Jesus, who invites but never pressures, leads but never forces, and always honors the pace of the wounded?

PART II

THE PROCESS OF HEALING

4

PREPARING THE GROUND

EVERY MINISTRY SESSION IS LIKE PLANTING A SEED. IF THE ground isn't prepared, the seed will not take root. You can have the best teaching, the clearest process, and the most powerful prayers, but if the soil of the session is not safe, ready, and receptive, the fruit will be limited.

That's why preparing the ground is so vital in inner healing. People are not projects—they are hearts. And hearts open slowly. They open when they feel safe, when they feel honored, and when the atmosphere makes space for the Spirit.

In this chapter, we'll talk about how to prepare that ground: building trust, taking a trauma-informed posture, inviting the Holy Spirit, and setting up the environment with consent.

Building Trust and Establishing Safety in the Session

Trust is the first door to inner healing. Without trust, people will not let you near their wounds. They may smile, they may nod, they may even pray with you—but their protectors will keep the real pain locked away. So how do you build trust?

- Be present. Give them your full attention. Don't check your phone, glance around the room, or act distracted. Look them in the eye. Show them that they matter.
- Listen well. Don't just wait for your turn to talk. Listen to understand. Reflect back what you hear. "So what I'm hearing is that when your dad left, you felt abandoned and unworthy." That tells them you are really paying attention.
- Honor their story. Never minimize pain. Don't compare it to others. Don't say, "At least it wasn't worse." Their pain is real, and it matters.
- Keep confidentiality. Let them know clearly: what they share will stay between you and the ministry team, unless there's a situation of danger that requires reporting. That assurance alone creates safety.
- Respect boundaries. If they don't want to share something, don't push. If they say they're not ready, honor that. Healing can only happen when people feel in control of their yes and no.

Trust is not built with one big moment—it's built with dozens of small signals that say, "You are safe here." When they feel safe, they will open.

Trauma-Informed Posture

To minister inner healing well, you must be trauma-informed. That doesn't mean you need a degree in counseling. It means you understand how trauma affects people, and you adjust your posture accordingly.

Trauma leaves people hyper-alert. Their nervous system is trained to scan for danger. Loud voices, sudden movements, or invasive questions can trigger that alarm system. That's why your posture must be gentle. Here are some trauma-informed principles:

- Go slow. Don't rush. Healing is not a race. If they only take one small step today, celebrate it.
- Stay calm. If they cry, shake, or even manifest, don't panic. Stay grounded. Your calmness helps regulate their nervous system.
- Use gentle language. Avoid harsh or aggressive tones. Speak with warmth and patience.
- Give choices. Trauma often steals choice. So give it back. "Would you like to pray out loud or silently?" "Are you comfortable closing your eyes, or do you want to keep them open?" Choices restore agency.
- Watch for triggers. Notice body language. If they tense up, freeze, or shut down, slow down. Ask, "How are you feeling right now?" Don't push past resistance—honor it.

Being trauma-informed doesn't mean you're walking on eggshells. It means you are tuned in. You are aware. You are shepherding hearts with wisdom and gentleness.

Inviting the Holy Spirit

No matter how skilled you are, no healing happens without the Holy Spirit. He is the Counselor. He is the Comforter. He is the Spirit of truth who leads people into freedom.

That's why every session begins with inviting Him. You don't assume He's just there—you acknowledge Him, welcome Him, and yield to Him.

A simple prayer works:

"Holy Spirit, we invite You into this time. Jesus, You are the Healer. We ask You to guide us, protect us, and minister Your love and truth. Have Your way."

This does three things:

1. Centers everyone on Jesus. It reminds both minister and recipient that this is His work, not ours.
2. Sets the atmosphere. The Spirit's presence shifts the environment from human effort to Kingdom power.
3. Opens hearts. When people hear you invite the Spirit, it helps them relax and expect Him to show up.

Sometimes, the Spirit may lead you differently than you expect. He may highlight a memory, surface an emotion, or give a picture. Stay sensitive. Don't force your agenda. Follow His.

Remember: you are not the healer—He is. Your job is to create the environment for Him to move.

Environment Setup

The physical environment matters more than many realize. If the room feels cold, chaotic, or unsafe, people will struggle to open their hearts. If the environment is peaceful, warm, and private, it creates safety. Here are some keys:

- Privacy. Make sure the space is free from interruptions. Turn off phones, silence notifications, and ensure no one will walk in unexpectedly.
- Comfort. Provide a comfortable chair. Have tissues available. Pay attention to lighting—too harsh can feel intimidating, too dim can feel unsafe.
- Order. A cluttered, messy room creates distraction. A clean, orderly space communicates care and intentionality.
- Accessibility. Make sure the room is easy to find and enter. Stress about logistics can block openness.

Think of the environment like setting the table. You're creating a space where someone can encounter Jesus without distraction or fear.

Consent

One of the most important principles in preparing the ground is consent. You never move forward without the person's permission. You don't assume. You don't push. You ask.

- Consent to pray. "Is it okay if we pray together right now?"
- Consent to ask Jesus. "Would you be open to inviting Jesus into this memory?"
- Consent to touch. "Would it be alright if I place my hand on your shoulder as we pray?"

Every step is an invitation, not a demand. Consent restores agency. It tells the person, "You are in control of your process. I am not here to overpower you—I am here to serve you."

When people know they can say no, they are far more likely

to say yes. And when they say yes, it's genuine. It's theirs. And Jesus meets them in that place of willingness.

Beyond Technique

Preparing the ground is not just about following steps—it's about carrying a spirit of honor. It's about saying with your presence, your tone, your setup, and your prayers: "You are safe. You are seen. You are loved. Jesus is here."

When people feel that, their walls come down. Their protectors begin to relax. Their hearts open. And in that place, Jesus can step in and heal what no human ever could.

Before every inner healing session, take the time to prepare the ground. Build trust. Carry a trauma-informed posture. Invite the Holy Spirit. Set up the environment with care. Ask for consent at every step.

These may seem like small details, but they are not. They are the difference between walls staying up and hearts opening. They are the difference between retraumatizing someone and seeing them healed. They are the difference between human effort and Kingdom transformation.

Remember: you are not just facilitating a meeting. You are hosting an encounter with Jesus. Prepare the ground well, and the Healer will do what only He can do.

Reflection Questions

1. HOW INTENTIONALLY DO I CULTIVATE SAFETY, TRUST, AND honor before I ever begin praying or ministering? Do people feel seen, heard, and valued when they sit with me? Which aspects of trust-building—presence, listening, honoring, confidentiality, respecting boundaries—come naturally, and which ones do I tend to overlook or rush through? What specific habits do I need to strengthen so the atmosphere I create consistently communicates, *"You are safe here"*?

2. IN WHAT WAYS DOES MY CURRENT POSTURE REFLECT A TRAUMA-informed, Spirit-led minister—and where do I need to grow in gentleness, awareness, and self-regulation? How aware am I of people's body language, emotional cues, or triggers? Do I sometimes rush, push, or lead with my agenda rather than the Spirit's pace? How might developing a calmer, more grounded presence help others regulate their fear or anxiety in a session?

3. HOW WELL DO I HONOR A PERSON'S AGENCY AND CONSENT—and what does my approach reveal about whether I'm truly serving or subtly controlling the process? Are there moments where I tend to assume rather than ask? How do I respond internally when someone hesitates, resists, or says they're not ready? What would it look like for me to fully honor their autonomy, slow down, and create space for a genuine yes that Jesus can move through?

5

IDENTIFYING THE WOUNDS

BEFORE YOU CAN MINISTER HEALING, YOU HAVE TO KNOW WHERE
the wounds are. A doctor doesn't prescribe medicine without
first examining the patient. In the same way, as inner healing
ministers, we don't just launch into prayers or declarations
without first discerning what is really going on in the soul.

Wounds are often buried deep. They are hidden beneath
behaviors, symptoms, and coping mechanisms. The person
may not even realize what's driving their pain. They may come
to you asking for freedom from anxiety, anger, or addiction, but
those are only the fruit. The root is almost always a wound—an
unhealed place in the soul where pain, lies, and trauma are still
alive.

This chapter is about learning to identify those wounds:
listening to the person's story, listening to the Spirit, recognizing shame and distorted identity, discerning performance
patterns, understanding intergenerational trauma, and asking
wise, Spirit-led questions that bring the roots to the surface.

Listening to Stories and the Spirit

Every person has a story. And in their story, you will hear the clues to their wounds. One of the most important skills for a minister is listening—not just hearing words, but truly listening. When you listen, pay attention to:

- Patterns. Do they keep circling back to rejection? To abandonment? To failure?
- Emotions. Do they choke up at certain points? Do they get angry when talking about a specific event?
- Gaps. Are there areas of silence or avoidance? Topics they skip quickly over?

Listening is not passive. It is active discernment. You are listening both to the person and to the Spirit. As they speak, you are also tuning your ear to what the Holy Spirit is highlighting. Sometimes you'll sense a nudge: "Ask more about their father." Or you'll feel a sudden compassion when they mention something quickly. Those nudges are often the Spirit pointing to the wound.

As ministers, we don't pry or dig. We don't interrogate. We listen with patience and love, and we follow the Spirit's lead.

Recognizing Shame Wounds and Distorted Identity

One of the deepest wounds people carry is shame. Shame is not the same as guilt. Guilt says, "I did something wrong." Shame says, "I am something wrong." Shame attacks identity. It convinces people they are unworthy, unlovable, or beyond redemption.

Shame wounds often come from abuse, rejection, or

neglect. A child who is constantly told they are stupid will eventually believe, "I am worthless." A woman who was molested may carry the lie, "I am dirty." A man abandoned by his father may believe, "I am unwanted."

You can recognize shame wounds when people use identity language:

- "I'm just a failure."
- "I'll never be good enough."
- "I'm not lovable."

These are not just thoughts—they are lies that have been written into their identity. Inner healing involves bringing those lies into the presence of Jesus and allowing Him to speak truth.

Shame is often hidden under layers of performance, anger, or withdrawal. That's why discernment is key. Don't take the outer behavior at face value. Ask the Spirit: "What is the lie underneath this?" When the shame wound is exposed, you can invite Jesus to heal it.

Identifying Performance and Perfectionism Patterns

Another common sign of inner wounds is performance. Many people live their whole lives trying to prove they are worthy. They strive for perfection, success, or approval because deep down they believe they are not enough. Performance patterns look like:

- Perfectionism. Always needing to get it exactly right, terrified of failure.
- Workaholism. Constantly busy, unable to rest.

- People-pleasing. Saying yes to everyone, afraid to disappoint.
- Religious striving. Trying to earn God's love through endless spiritual activity.

These patterns are not just personality quirks. They are indicators of wounds. Usually, they trace back to a root of rejection or conditional love. A child who only received affection when they performed well may grow up believing, "I am only valuable if I succeed."

As ministers, we must learn to recognize performance not as strength but as a symptom of brokenness. Behind the overachiever is often a scared child still trying to earn love. Inner healing helps them lay down performance and receive unconditional love from the Father.

Intergenerational Trauma: Recognizing Inherited Family Pain

Not all wounds start with the person in front of you. Many are inherited from previous generations. Scripture speaks clearly about this dynamic. Exodus 20:5 says that the sins of the fathers can affect the children to the third and fourth generation. While Christ breaks every curse at the cross, the patterns often remain until they are specifically renounced and healed. Intergenerational trauma can look like:

- Addiction patterns. Alcoholism, drug use, gambling, or sexual sin running through the family line.
- Abuse cycles. Children of abusers often become abusers unless the cycle is broken.
- Mental health struggles. Patterns of depression, anxiety, or fear passed down.

- Abandonment. Generations of fathers walking out on their families.
- Religious bondage. Legalism, control, or occult involvement handed down.

You may hear someone say, "This has always been in our family." That's a clue. Intergenerational trauma is real. And inner healing is the place where Jesus breaks the cycle.

Part of identifying wounds is helping people see that what they are carrying may not have started with them. When they recognize it as an inherited pattern, they can repent, renounce, and step into the freedom Jesus purchased for them.

Asking Wise, Spirit-Led Questions

One of the most effective tools in identifying wounds is asking questions. But not just any questions—wise, Spirit-led questions.

Bad questions feel invasive, controlling, or prying. Good questions feel honoring, curious, and open. They help the person explore their story without feeling pressured. Here are some examples:

- "When you feel this fear, what does it remind you of?"
- "If you had to put words to the lie you believe about yourself, what would it be?"
- "When was the first time you remember feeling that way?"
- "Did anyone ever say something to you that made you believe this about yourself?"

- "How did your mom or dad respond to you when you were hurting?"

These questions are not formulas. They are tools. The key is to stay dependent on the Spirit. Sometimes He will give you a specific question that unlocks the wound. Sometimes He will nudge you to stay silent and let the person process.

Always remember: the goal is not to dig up pain for its own sake. The goal is to bring the wound into the light so Jesus can heal it.

Discernment and Sensitivity

Identifying wounds requires discernment. You cannot always take everything at face value. People may tell you one story, but the real wound is underneath. They may focus on surface problems, but the Spirit will highlight the root.

At the same time, you must be sensitive. If you push too hard, you can retraumatize. If you assume too much, you can miss what God is really doing. Balance discernment with gentleness. Be willing to wait. Trust that the Holy Spirit knows the perfect moment to surface the wound.

Finding the Root

If you want to see lasting healing, you have to find the root. Surface solutions never work. Band-aids don't heal deep cuts. You must identify the wound—the lie, the shame, the trauma, the generational pattern—before you can bring Jesus into it.

As ministers, our role is not to diagnose like doctors but to discern like shepherds. We listen to stories. We listen to the

Spirit. We recognize shame, performance, and generational pain. We ask wise questions. And when the wound comes into the light, we don't try to fix it ourselves. We invite the Healer.

That's the beauty of this ministry. We don't have to know everything. We don't have to be experts in psychology. We just have to be faithful to listen, discern, and lead people to Jesus. He is the one who binds up the brokenhearted. He is the one who restores the soul. And it all begins with identifying the wounds.

Reflection Questions

1. HOW WELL DO I LISTEN—BOTH TO THE PERSON'S STORY AND TO the Holy Spirit—and what hinders me from hearing beneath the surface?When someone shares their story, do I tend to focus on their words, or am I attentive to what's beneath the words? What distractions, assumptions, or internal "fixer" tendencies sometimes keep me from truly listening? How can I grow in partnering with the Spirit so that I recognize His subtle prompts, questions, or moments of compassion that reveal the real wound?

2. WHAT SIGNS OF SHAME, PERFORMANCE, PERFECTIONISM, OR generational patterns do I tend to overlook—either in others or in myself? When ministering, am I more prone to address the surface behaviors (anxiety, anger, addiction) rather than the roots? Which symptoms of shame or performance do I personally resonate with—and how might that shape (or distort) the way I discern them in others? How can I invite the Spirit to help me see identity lies, inherited patterns, and deeper roots with greater clarity and compassion?

3. HOW COMFORTABLE AM I WITH ASKING SPIRIT-LED QUESTIONS instead of offering solutions—and what does that reveal about my posture as a minister? Do I tend to rush into teaching, correcting, or fixing instead of gently guiding with questions? How willing am I to sit in silence, wait, and let the Spirit lead the process rather than steering it myself? In what ways can I grow in asking questions that open doors instead of questions that push or pry?

6

PRESENTING JESUS IN THE PAIN — THE SOZO MODEL

INNER HEALING ISN'T ABOUT CLEVER WORDS; IT'S ABOUT BRINGING the Living Jesus into the place where the soul was wounded and letting Him minister directly. The model we use at SOZO is simple, relational, and powerful: we present Jesus in the memory, listen for His truth, obey what He shows us, and follow Him through forgiveness, integration, and exchange.

Think of this chapter as a field guide. I'll give you the exact flow I use, with sample language you can adopt. Be faithful to the Spirit, keep the pace gentle, and never push people beyond what they're ready for.

The Heart Posture (Before Any Steps)

- Honor and consent: "We'll go at your pace. If anything feels too much, say so. We'll stop and ask Jesus what to do."
- Safety and dignity: You're not digging for details; you're following Jesus. No graphic probing, no pressure.

- Dependence on the Spirit: "Holy Spirit, You are the Counselor. Lead us."

Step 1 — Enter the Memory (Locate the Wound)

Gently help the person name and enter the place where pain is still alive.
Your language:

- "What's going on? Can you describe the scene that's coming up?"
- "About how old are you in this memory?"
- "What are the main emotions you're feeling right now?"
- "Are there any lies you're believing about yourself, God, or others in this moment?"

Notes

- If they can't name the lie yet, ask: "If there were a lie here, what might it be?"
- You're gathering the "address" (time, place), "temperature" (emotions), and "intruder" (lies).

Pace: Slow. Keep your voice gentle. Validate: "That makes sense." "Thank you for trusting me."

Step 2 — Ask Permission for Jesus to Enter

We honor will. We never force encounters.
Your language:

- "Would you like to invite Jesus into this memory with you?"

- (If yes) "Jesus, we invite You right here, right now."

If they hesitate: "No problem. We can wait. Jesus, what would bring safety here?" Sometimes He'll give you a picture, a word, or a sense (like His hand on their shoulder). Follow that.

Step 3 — Help Them Notice Jesus

We anchor the encounter in awareness of His presence.
Your language:

- "Can you see Jesus? Or sense/know He's here?
  (Seeing isn't required—some feel or simply know.)"
- "Where is He in the scene?"
- "What is He doing right now?"

If they can't see Him: Normalize it.

"Many people don't see images but they sense or know. Ask Jesus, 'Where are You?' and tell me the first sense that comes."

If they sense darkness, invite light: "Jesus, shine Your light here." If they sense distance, invite closeness: "Jesus, come nearer."

Step 4 — Ask Jesus About the Emotions and Lies

We let Jesus define reality in the moment of pain.
Your language:

- "Jesus, do they have to feel this way now that You are here?"
- "Jesus, what do You say about the lie they're believing?"

- To the person: "What are you noticing as He speaks? Any shift in your heart, body, or the scene?"

Encourage short answers; don't over-explain. If they hear nothing, ask: "What's the next true thing you do know about Jesus here?" Build on the smallest truth.

Step 5 — Ask Jesus About Forgiveness (Build Compassion)

We don't force forgiveness. We invite Jesus to lead it. Your language:

- "Jesus, is there anyone we need to forgive connected to this memory?"
- "If so, would You help us understand what was going on with that person—without excusing sin—so we can find compassion to forgive?"

Let Jesus give perspective (brokenness, deception, generational pain). Compassion makes forgiveness possible without denying the harm.

Leading forgiveness:

"Lord, I choose to forgive [name] for [what they did] and for how it made me feel [name the emotions]. I release them from my judgment and give them to You. Heal my heart."

Guardrail

- No graphic retelling. Keep confessions brief and non-descriptive.
- If emotions surge, slow down, breathe, remind: "Jesus is here."

Step 6 — Release the Person from the Memory

We complete forgiveness with a picture of release.
Your language:

- "Now, see Jesus standing between you and [person]."
- "When you're ready, release them—watch them leave the memory with Jesus present."

If they struggle, ask: "Jesus, what would help them release this?" Sometimes He gives a symbolic action (handing over a letter, undoing a rope, closing a door).

Step 7 — Address Protectors and Child Parts

Protectors are survival parts that guard pain. We honor them and lead them to Jesus.
Your language:

- "Jesus, is there any protector connected to this memory?"
- "If so, we honor you, protector. Thank you for trying to keep us safe. We bless you.
- Would you go be with Jesus now and let Him carry what you've carried?"

Invite the person to speak to that part:

- "I see you. Thank you. You don't have to keep doing this. Go be with Jesus."

If there's resistance: "Jesus, what does this protector need to feel safe going with You?" Follow what He shows—often it's assurance they won't be abandoned.

Step 8 — Minister to the Child and Integrate

This is the tender moment you described: adult self meets the younger self with Jesus present.
Your language:

- "Now, see your present-day self step into the scene with Jesus."
- "Go to your younger self. Give them a hug."
- "Say whatever they most needed to hear then:
- 'It's going to be okay. It wasn't your fault. I'm here now. You're not alone.'"
- "Now, watch Jesus hug both of you."

Integration:

- "Jesus, would You heal the child and bring wholeness?"
- "When you're ready, see the child gently absorb into your present self—no parts lost, just wholeness restored."

If they can't integrate yet, don't force it. Ask: "Jesus, what is the next step toward safety and wholeness?" Sometimes the child part goes with Jesus for a season. That's okay.

Step 9 — The Holy Exchange (Give and Receive)

We trade burdens for gifts. This seals the encounter.
Your language:

- "Jesus, what do You want them to give You from this memory? (shame, fear, anger, guilt...)"

- "Now, Jesus, what do You want to give them in exchange? (peace, purity, courage, belonging...)"
- "Receive it. Describe it if you can—what does it look or feel like?"

Let them breathe, notice bodily shifts (warmth, lightness, peace). These embodied changes matter.

Step 10 — Close the Memory with Jesus

We honor completion. We don't slam the door; we walk out with Him.
Your language:

- "Now, see you and Jesus turn and leave that memory together.
- The door remains redeemed, not erased—He owns it now."
- "Holy Spirit, seal this in Your peace."

Invite a deep breath. Offer water. Give a moment of quiet thanksgiving.

Sample Session Flow (All Together)

1. "What's happening? How old are you? What emotions and lies are here?"
2. "Would you like to invite Jesus into this memory?"
3. "Can you see/sense Him? Where is He? What is He doing?"
4. "Jesus, do they have to feel this way now that You're here? What do You say about the lie?"
5. "Jesus, is there anyone they need to forgive? Would You help us see what was going on with them?"

6. → Lead forgiveness and release.
7. "Jesus, are there protectors connected to this? Protector, thank you. Go be with Jesus."
8. "Step in as your present self. Hug your younger self. Say what they needed to hear. Watch Jesus hug you both."
9. → "Jesus, heal the child." (Integration if ready.)
10. "Jesus, what do they need to give You? What do You want to give them?"
11. "See you and Jesus leave the memory together."
12. Seal in prayer and peace.

Troubleshooting & Gentle Alternatives

"I can't see anything."

- Normalize: "Many don't see but they sense or know. Ask, 'Jesus, where are You?' and tell me the first sense that comes."
- Offer anchors: "Do you feel a shift—warmth, breath, calm?"
- Use Scripture as focus: picture Jesus as the Good Shepherd entering the scene.

Numbness or shutdown.

- Grounding: "Notice your feet on the floor, your breath in your chest." Invite a 4–6 breath pattern (inhale 4, exhale 6).
- Ask permission to pause and pray: "Holy Spirit, bring Your calm."
- Don't force. Sometimes the next step is simply Jesus placing His hand on their shoulder—stay there.

Overwhelm or flashback.

- Slow everything down. "Jesus, turn down the volume."
- Re-orient: "You're here with me now. It's 20—. You're safe."
- If needed, postpone deep work and simply receive peace. You can return later.

Sexual abuse memories.

- Keep language non-graphic.
- Move quickly to Jesus' presence, truth, and dignity.
- Maintain strong boundaries and accountability in the room.

A spirit manifests.

- Don't panic. Bind and quiet it briefly: "I bind every interfering spirit; you will be silent."
- If it continues, pivot per your training (see chapter on Inner Healing vs. Deliverance).
- After deliverance, you can return to the memory for healing if appropriate.

Integration not ready.

- Let Jesus hold the child part for now. "Jesus, keep them safe with You."
- Healing is a process. Celebrate progress.

Language You Can Use (Quick Prompts)

- Entering: "What's happening? How old are you? What emotions and lies are here?"
- Invite: "Jesus, we invite You into this memory now."
- Notice: "Where are You, Jesus? What are You doing?"
- Truth: "Jesus, do they have to feel this way now that You're here? What do You say about this lie?"
- Forgive: "Jesus, who do they need to forgive? Show us what was going on with them so we can find compassion."
- Release: "I forgive __ for __ and how it made me feel __. I release them to You."
- Protectors: "Protector, we honor you. Go be with Jesus."
- Child: "Present-you, hug younger-you. Say what they needed to hear. Jesus, hug them both."
- Integrate: "Jesus, heal the child. When ready, bring wholeness."
- Exchange: "Jesus, what do they give You? What do You give them?"
- Close: "Walk out with Jesus. Holy Spirit, seal this."

Guardrails That Keep Everyone Safe

- Consent at every turn. Ask before each movement.
- No pressure. If they can't or won't, you wait. The Spirit knows the pace.
- No graphic probing. We follow the Spirit, not curiosity.
- Minister with a helper present. Especially with cross-gender ministry.
- Confidentiality. Protect their story.
- Referrals when needed. Severe trauma may require professional partnership. We honor that.

After the Encounter: Stabilize and Anchor

- Offer water. Check their body: "How do you feel?"
- Give Scripture anchors to reinforce the truth Jesus spoke (write them down).
- Encourage a brief gratitude prayer: "Jesus, thank You for what You did."
- Assign a simple practice: each day this week, ask, "Jesus, remind me what You gave me," and receive it again.

Why This Works

Because Jesus is alive. He is Lord over time, memory, pain, and identity. When He steps into a wounded place, the lie loses power. The emotions shift under His presence. Forgiveness becomes possible. Protectors find rest. The child is healed. And the person walks out with Him—whole.

You don't need to force breakthroughs. You host His presence and follow His lead. This keeps the ministry pure, safe, and powerful.

Closing Prayer

"Jesus, You are the Healer of the soul. Teach us to present You with reverence and simplicity. Make our rooms safe, our language gentle, our pace Spirit-led. Guard us from pressure and pride. Give us eyes to see You in the memory, hearts to listen to Your truth, and courage to follow You through forgiveness, integration, and exchange. Seal this model in us, and make it fruitful for many. Amen."

Reflection Questions

1. How well do I personally embody the heart posture required for this model, before I ever begin using the steps? When I think about entering someone's deepest wounds, do I truly feel a sense of reverence, humility, and tenderness? Do I naturally create an atmosphere where people feel in control, respected, and safe—or do I sometimes rush, direct, or assume? Which aspects of my posture most align with Jesus' way of ministering, and which ones need to be surrendered, refined, or healed?

2. What parts of this model do I feel most confident in, and which parts stir fear, discomfort, or uncertainty in me? Which step feels natural for me, and why? Which step feels hardest—entering memories, listening for Jesus, approaching forgiveness, addressing protectors, or facilitating the exchange? What does my comfort or discomfort reveal about where I still need Jesus to meet me, teach me, or heal me?

3. How deeply do I trust that Jesus Himself will minister in the memory—and where am I still tempted to rely on my own skill, words, or control? When I imagine sitting with someone in pain, do I trust that Jesus will show up, speak, reveal, and heal—or do I feel pressure to make something happen? Where do I still carry fear that I won't "get it right," won't hear God clearly, or won't be able to help? What would it look like for me to minister from a place of quiet confidence in Jesus' presence rather than human effort?

7

FORGIVENESS AND RELEASE

IF THERE IS ONE DOORWAY THAT LEADS MORE PEOPLE INTO freedom than any other, it is forgiveness. Nothing keeps people bound in pain, torment, and lies like unforgiveness. Nothing opens the way for healing, peace, and wholeness like forgiveness.

Forgiveness is not a suggestion—it's a command of Jesus. But it's also a gift. It is not about excusing evil or pretending something didn't hurt. It is about releasing the person, releasing the debt, and letting God be the Judge. Forgiveness sets the prisoner free, and often the prisoner was you.

In this chapter, I want to help you as a minister understand what forgiveness is and what it is not, how to walk people through forgiving others, forgiving themselves, and even releasing anger toward God. We'll also look at specific wounds —like father and mother wounds, and betrayal wounds—that require deep forgiveness. Finally, I'll give you practical prayers and release exercises you can use.

Forgiving Others

Jesus made forgiveness non-negotiable. In Matthew 6:14–15 He said,

> *"For if you forgive men their trespasses, your heavenly Father will also forgive you. But if you do not forgive men their trespasses, neither will your Father forgive your trespasses."*

That's heavy. But Jesus knew how dangerous unforgiveness is.

When we hold onto unforgiveness, we stay tied to the person and the pain. It's like carrying them around on our back. Every time we rehearse the memory, the wound stays fresh. Demons love to feed on unforgiveness. It gives them legal ground to torment.

Forgiving others does not mean:

- Saying what they did was okay.
- Saying you have to reconcile with them.
- Saying you'll trust them again.

Forgiveness means:

- You release them from your judgment.
- You hand their case over to God.
- You choose to cancel the debt, even if the feelings take time to catch up.

Practical language:

> *"Lord, I choose to forgive [name] for [what they did] and for how it*

made me feel [list emotions]. I release them to You. I cancel their debt.
They owe me nothing. Heal my heart, Lord."

Forgiving Self

Many people find it harder to forgive themselves than to forgive others. They live under shame, regret, and self-condemnation. They replay their mistakes and failures, punishing themselves over and over.

But forgiveness of self is part of receiving the gospel. If Jesus has forgiven you, who are you to withhold forgiveness from yourself? To hold onto self-hatred is to say His blood wasn't enough.

Practical language:

"Lord, I choose to forgive myself for [what I did]. I release myself
from judgment. I receive the blood of Jesus as full payment. I agree
with Your truth that I am forgiven, clean, and free."

As a minister, you may need to help people speak forgiveness out loud over themselves. Often it feels awkward, but it is powerful. When they hear their own voice releasing themselves, shame loses its grip.

Releasing Anger at God

This one trips many people up. Theologically, we know God never sins. He never does wrong. He doesn't need forgiveness. But experientially, people often carry anger or disappointment toward God. They feel like He abandoned them, failed them, or let them suffer.

If you tell them, "You can't be mad at God," they'll shut

down. But if you create space for them to release their anger to Him, healing can flow.

Practical language:

"God, I felt like You let me down when [event]. I've carried anger and disappointment toward You. I release that to You now. I give You my questions and my pain. I choose to trust that You are good, even when I don't understand."

It's not about forgiving God—it's about releasing Him from false accusations in their heart. It's about clearing away the offense so intimacy can be restored.

Father Wounds and Mother Wounds

One of the deepest areas of unforgiveness is toward parents. Fathers and mothers shape how we see the world, how we see ourselves, and how we see God. When they wound us—through absence, neglect, abuse, or harshness—the impact is profound.

Father Wounds

A father's role is to provide identity, protection, and affirmation. When fathers fail in these areas, children grow up insecure, rejected, or angry.

Signs of father wounds:

- Striving to prove worth.
- Difficulty trusting authority.
- Struggle seeing God as Father.

Forgiveness here is critical. People need to forgive their fathers for not being who they needed them to be.

Practical language:

"Father, I forgive you for not being there for me. I forgive you for your anger, for your absence, for not affirming me. I release you from my judgment. I let go of the debt I thought you owed me."

Mother Wounds

A mother's role is to nurture, comfort, and create belonging. When mothers wound—through control, criticism, or neglect—it leaves deep marks.

Signs of mother wounds:

- Struggle receiving comfort.
- Feeling unsafe in relationships.
- Struggle trusting women or female authority.

Forgiveness here involves releasing the mother from unmet expectations and pain.

Practical language:

"Mom, I forgive you for not nurturing me, for your criticism, for your control. I release you. I let go of the pain and the lies I believed. I give you to Jesus."

Betrayal and Trust Wounds

Few wounds cut deeper than betrayal. When someone close breaks trust, it can shatter the soul. David wrote in Psalm 55:12–14,

"For it is not an enemy who reproaches me; then I could bear it... but it was you, a man my equal, my companion and my acquaintance.

We took sweet counsel together, and walked to the house of God in the throng."

Betrayal wounds make people cynical, closed, and suspicious. They swear inner vows like, "I'll never trust again." Those vows must be broken.

Forgiveness here is often a process. People may need to forgive layer by layer. Encourage them not to wait until they feel like it. Forgiveness is a choice of the will. The feelings usually follow.
Practical language:

"Lord, I forgive [name] for betraying me. I forgive them for breaking trust. I release the bitterness, the anger, and the vow I made never to trust again. Heal my heart and teach me how to trust with wisdom."

Practical Forgiveness Prayers and Release Exercises

Here are some tools you can use in sessions:

General Forgiveness Prayer

"Lord, I choose to forgive [name] for [specific action] and for how it made me feel [emotions]. I cancel their debt. I release them into Your hands. Heal my heart."

Forgiving Self

"Lord, I forgive myself for [what I did]. I receive Your forgiveness. I declare that I am clean, forgiven, and free because of the blood of Jesus."

Releasing Anger at God

"God, I give You my anger and disappointment over [event]. I release You from the false accusations in my heart. I choose to trust that You are good."

The Empty Chair Exercise

Have the person picture the offender sitting in a chair. Lead them to speak forgiveness directly: "I forgive you for... I release you." Then have them see Jesus standing between them, taking the offender away.

The Debt Release Exercise

Ask: "What do you feel this person owes you?" (Love, protection, apology, affirmation?) Then have them say: "I release you from owing me [that thing]. I cancel the debt. I give it to Jesus."

Common Obstacles to Forgiveness

- "I don't feel like it." Forgiveness is a decision, not a feeling.
- "They don't deserve it." Neither did we, yet Christ forgave us.
- "If I forgive, they'll get away with it." No—they answer to God. Forgiveness releases you, not them.
- "I already forgave, but it still hurts." Sometimes forgiveness is a process. Keep releasing until the pain lessens.

The Freedom of Forgiveness

Forgiveness is not easy. It costs. But it costs less than

carrying bitterness for a lifetime. Unforgiveness chains you to the past. Forgiveness opens the door to freedom.

As a minister, your role is to gently lead people into forgiveness—not by shaming or pressuring them, but by helping them see that it is possible with Jesus. Invite Him into the memory, ask Him to give compassion, and then lead them to release the debt.

When they forgive, you'll often see it instantly: their face softens, their body relaxes, tears flow, peace comes. That's the power of forgiveness. And it is central to inner healing.

Reflection Questions

1. WHERE IN MY OWN LIFE DO I STILL HOLD UNFORGIVENESS toward others, myself, or God? How is that unresolved pain shaping the way I minister to others? Who comes to mind—parent, friend, leader, betrayer, or even yourself—when you consider the word "unforgiveness"? How has holding onto that wound affected your emotions, relationships, trust, or view of God? What would it look like for you to release that debt to Jesus today—not because the person deserves it, but because you want freedom?

2. WHAT LIES, VOWS, OR EXPECTATIONS ARE HIDING UNDERNEATH my resistance to forgiving certain people or certain memories? What do you feel someone *owes* you that keeps you holding onto the pain? Are there inner vows or statements you made in the moment of hurt that still shape your behavior today? How might breaking those vows and releasing those debts create space for healing, peace, and new identity?

3. HOW PREPARED AM I TO GUIDE OTHERS THROUGH FORGIVENESS with gentleness, honor, and wisdom—especially in areas like parent wounds, betrayal, or anger toward God? When someone shares a deep betrayal or parent wound, do you feel confident, hesitant, overwhelmed, or unsure of how to lead them toward forgiveness? What strengths do you already carry as a minister in this area, and what specific areas do you need Jesus to deepen, mature, or equip in you?

8

BREAKING INNER VOWS AND LIES

ONE OF THE MOST SUBTLE BUT POWERFUL FORMS OF BONDAGE IN people's lives is the inner vow. Many don't even know they've made them, yet these vows drive their choices, their emotions, their relationships, and their walk with God. Paired with inner vows are ungodly beliefs—the lies that become the lens through which people see themselves and the world.

If forgiveness heals wounds of the past, breaking inner vows and lies untangles the knots that keep people bound in the present. Unless these vows and lies are exposed, repented of, and replaced with truth, a person can experience forgiveness yet still walk in cycles of defeat.

In this chapter, we'll unpack what vows are and how they form, explore common ungodly beliefs tied to vows, and then walk through how to break them with repentance, renunciation, and truth. I'll also give you practical prayers to lead people into freedom.

What Are Inner Vows?

An inner vow is a promise or decision a person makes in response to pain, fear, or trauma. It is usually subconscious. At the moment of wounding, the person makes a decision to protect themselves from being hurt again. Examples:

- A child who was abandoned may say, "I'll never depend on anyone again."
- A teenager mocked for failure may say, "I'll never try unless I know I'll win."
- A girl whose father was harsh may say, "I'll never let a man control me."
- A boy shamed by his mother may say, "I'll never let anyone close enough to hurt me."

On the surface, vows feel protective. But in reality, they become prisons. They lock people into patterns of fear, isolation, control, or perfectionism. Instead of being free to respond to God's Spirit, they are controlled by a vow they made years ago.

Jesus warned about making oaths in Matthew 5:34–37. Why? Because our words carry power. Proverbs 18:21 says, "Death and life are in the power of the tongue." Inner vows are agreements with death. They release bondage, not freedom.

How Inner Vows Form

Inner vows almost always form in moments of trauma or repeated patterns of pain. The child is hurt, and rather than bring that pain to God, they try to solve it themselves. They make a decision that becomes a spiritual contract.

The process looks like this:

1. Wound occurs. Abuse, rejection, betrayal, neglect, shame.
2. Lie is believed. "I'm not safe." "I'm unlovable." "I'll always be rejected."
3. Vow is made. "I'll never trust anyone again." "I'll always prove I'm better."
4. Behavior follows. Walls go up, striving begins, control takes over.

Years later, the person may not even remember making the vow, but the vow is still active. The enemy uses it as a legal right to keep them bound.

Common Ungodly Beliefs Tied to Vows

Inner vows don't stand alone—they are tied to ungodly beliefs. The vow is the decision, the belief is the lie.

Here are some common ones:

- Vow: "I'll never need anyone."
- Lie: "People always abandon me. I'm on my own."
- Vow: "I'll never forgive them."
- Lie: "If I forgive, I'll lose control and get hurt again."
- Vow: "I'll always be the strong one."
- Lie: "Weakness makes me worthless."
- Vow: "I'll never let myself cry."
- Lie: "Emotions are dangerous. Vulnerability equals pain."
- Vow: "I'll never be like my parents."
- Lie: "My worth is defined by avoiding their mistakes."
- Vow: "I'll only trust myself."
- Lie: "No one else is safe. Even God can't be trusted."

These ungodly beliefs become filters. They distort how people hear God, how they see others, and how they interpret life. The vow cements the lie.

Why Vows Are Dangerous

Inner vows are dangerous because they:

- Block intimacy. They prevent people from letting others in.
- Fuel control. They drive people to manage every situation.
- Hinder trust. They make it difficult to trust God or authority.
- Cause cycles. The very thing they try to avoid, they often recreate.
- Give demons access. Vows create agreements the enemy can exploit.

For example, someone who vows, "I'll never be poor," may become consumed with greed or workaholism. Someone who vows, "I'll never be like my dad," may end up repeating his patterns. The vow attracts what it tries to avoid. That's why vows must be broken—not just ignored.

Breaking Inner Vows: Repentance, Renunciation, Replacement

Freedom comes when people recognize the vow, repent for making it, renounce it, and replace it with truth.

Step 1: Recognition

Help the person identify the vow. Ask:

- "When did you first start feeling this way?"
- "Did you ever say to yourself, 'I'll never...' or 'I'll always...'?"
- "What decision did you make to protect yourself?"

Step 2: Repentance

Repentance is acknowledging the vow was sin. It was self-protection instead of God-dependence.

Prayer:
"Lord, I repent for making this vow. I repent for trusting in myself instead of You. Forgive me."

Step 3: Renunciation

Renunciation is breaking agreement.

Prayer:
"In the name of Jesus, I renounce the vow I made that [repeat vow]. I break agreement with it. It no longer defines me."

Step 4: Replacement with Truth

Always replace the lie with God's truth.

Prayer:
"Jesus, what is Your truth for me instead?"

(Wait for them to hear/see what He gives. It may be Scripture, a phrase, or an image.)

Then have them declare it out loud:

"I receive the truth that [truth statement]."

Practical Renunciation Prayers

Here are some examples you can use:

- Vow: "I'll never trust anyone."
- Prayer: "Lord, I repent for vowing never to trust. I renounce that vow. I declare the truth that I am safe in You and can build healthy trust with others."
- Vow: "I'll never forgive."
- Prayer: "Lord, I repent for vowing never to forgive. I renounce that vow. I declare the truth that I forgive as I have been forgiven."
- Vow: "I'll always be strong."
- Prayer: "Lord, I repent for vowing to always be strong in my own strength. I renounce that vow. I declare the truth that Your strength is made perfect in my weakness."
- Vow: "I'll never cry."
- Prayer: "Lord, I repent for vowing never to cry. I renounce that vow. I declare the truth that You created my emotions, and I am safe to feel and heal."
- Vow: "I'll never be like my parents."
- Prayer: "Lord, I repent for vowing never to be like my parents. I renounce that vow. I declare the truth that I am defined by You, not by their failures."

Minister's Role in Breaking Vows

As a minister, your job is not to identify every vow for the person. Your role is to create space, ask questions, and listen to the Spirit. Often the Holy Spirit will surface the exact phrase of the vow.

Encourage the person to speak the vow out loud as they renounce it. There is power in naming it and then declaring it broken. Then, emphasize replacing it with truth. If the vow is removed but not replaced, the lie will creep back in.

Be patient. Some people carry dozens of vows. Don't rush to break them all in one session. Focus on the ones the Spirit highlights. Trust that healing is a journey.

Testimonies of Freedom

I've seen incredible freedom when vows are broken. I've seen marriages healed when spouses renounced vows of self-protection. I've seen leaders freed from perfectionism when they renounced vows of striving. I've seen people who couldn't cry for decades finally weep in safety after breaking vows against emotions.

These are not small shifts. They are life-changing. And they are available to anyone willing to repent, renounce, and receive truth.

The Power of Truth

At the end of the day, inner vows and lies are agreements with darkness. They keep people bound. But the cross is stronger. The blood of Jesus cancels every vow. The truth of Jesus replaces every lie.

As a minister, your role is to help people see the vow, break the agreement, and step into truth. Keep it simple. Keep it Spirit-led.

When the vow is broken, the lie loses power. When the lie is replaced, the truth sets them free. And when Jesus speaks truth into that place, the person is no longer controlled by a decision they made in fear—they are free to live as a son or daughter of God.

Reflection Questions

1. WHAT INNER VOWS OR SELF-PROTECTIVE DECISIONS HAVE I made in moments of hurt, fear, or rejection—and how have these vows shaped my relationships, identity, and walk with God? Inner vows often hide beneath behaviors like control, perfectionism, isolation, or distrust. Are there recurring patterns in your life that might trace back to a vow ("I'll never...", "I'll always...")? What event or person was connected to that vow being formed? How has that vow influenced the way you love, trust, receive, or relate to God and others today?

2. WHAT UNGODLY BELIEFS HAVE BECOME THE LENS THROUGH which I interpret life—and how have these lies limited my freedom, identity, and ability to receive truth from Jesus? Ungodly beliefs attach themselves to vows and become filters that distort reality. What lies about yourself do you often find playing in your mind? What lies about God or people feel "true," even though Scripture says otherwise? How would your life look different if Jesus replaced these beliefs with His truth?

3. HOW READY AM I TO BRING THESE VOWS TO JESUS—REPENTING, renouncing, and replacing them with truth—and what resistance, fear, or hesitation do I still need to surrender? Breaking vows requires vulnerability, humility, and trust. Do you feel resistance at the thought of repenting for a vow—because it once felt protective? What fears arise when you consider trusting God instead of your vow? What would it look like for you to fully embrace the truth Jesus wants to give you in exchange?

9

HEALING FRAGMENTED PARTS AND DISSOCIATION

ONE OF THE MOST MISUNDERSTOOD AREAS OF INNER HEALING IS fragmentation and dissociation. For some, the very idea that a soul can fragment or that a person can have different "parts" feels strange or unbiblical. But when you sit with survivors of deep trauma, ritual abuse, or repeated violations, you see the reality: the soul often splits as a way of surviving overwhelming pain.

As ministers of healing, we need to be equipped to recognize fragmentation, understand dissociation, and carry the compassion of Jesus into places that feel impossible. We are not dealing with mental illness in the way the world defines it—we are dealing with hearts that have been shattered and need the Shepherd to gather the pieces.

This chapter will unpack what fragmentation looks like, how dissociation manifests, the role of protectors, the challenge of evil alters, and how to walk with people through the process of healing and integration.

Soul Fragmentation: How It Looks and Why It Happens

The soul is made up of mind, will, and emotions. When trauma comes—especially in childhood—the soul sometimes fragments as a way to protect itself. The child cannot process the pain, so the soul creates compartments. One part carries the memory. Another carries the emotions. Another carries the function of daily life.

This is not weakness. It is survival. A child who is abused may "leave" mentally in order to survive the moment. That part of their soul stays stuck in the trauma while the rest moves on. Years later, those parts may still be frozen in fear, shame, or rage.

Signs of fragmentation:

- Sudden mood shifts with no clear reason.
- Feeling like "part of me" is still a child.
- Gaps in memory or lost time.
- Strong emotional reactions that feel disproportionate.
- Hearing "inside voices" that are not demonic but carry parts of self.

Psalm 23 speaks of the Lord as Shepherd who "restores my soul." That word "restore" means to bring back, to gather, to heal what is scattered. Fragmentation is not the end of the story. Jesus restores.

Dissociation Disorders: Recognition and Ministry Posture

In clinical terms, dissociation is the disconnection of thoughts, memories, or sense of identity. It can be mild—like daydreaming—or severe—like Dissociative Identity Disorder

(DID). As ministers, we are not diagnosing, but we must recognize patterns so we can minister wisely.

Common forms of dissociation:

- Depersonalization. Feeling detached from one's body, as if watching from outside.
- Derealization. Feeling the world around you is unreal or dreamlike.
- Dissociative Amnesia. Inability to recall traumatic events.
- Dissociative Identity Disorder (DID). Presence of distinct identity states or parts that take control at different times.

When you encounter dissociation in ministry:

- Stay calm. Don't panic. Dissociation is a survival strategy.
- Honor the person. Don't label them as crazy or broken. They are precious to God.
- Invite Jesus. He can reach parts of the soul we cannot.
- Don't force integration. Healing is a process. Jesus knows the pace.

Remember, trauma created dissociation to protect. The same God who designed the soul knows how to restore it.

Protectors: Roles, Behaviors, How to Engage

Protectors are parts of the soul that form to guard against future pain. They may be angry, controlling, numb, or hypervigilant. Their job is to keep the person from being hurt again.

Signs of protectors:

- Aggressive inner voices saying, "Don't trust them."
- Walls of numbness that shut down emotions.
- Perfectionism or control that refuses vulnerability.
- Fearful parts that refuse to let the memory surface.

As ministers, we never fight protectors. We honor them. We recognize their role. We thank them for trying to keep the person safe. Then we invite them to meet Jesus.

Practical language:

"Protector, we honor you for the role you've played in trying to keep [name] safe. Thank you for your hard work. But you don't have to carry this anymore. Will you go to Jesus now and let Him carry what you've been carrying?"

Often protectors are relieved to release the burden. When they encounter Jesus, they realize He can do what they never could.

Evil Alters: Discerning Demonic Contamination vs. Trauma Parts

Not every part of the soul is simply human. Sometimes, in the midst of severe trauma—especially ritual abuse—demons attach themselves to fragments. These become what we call "evil alters." They are not true parts of the soul but trauma parts contaminated or overshadowed by demonic presence.

How to discern the difference:

- Trauma part: Speaks with fear, sadness, or confusion. Motivated by survival.

- Evil alter: Speaks with hatred, blasphemy, or cruelty. Motivated by destruction.

Both require compassion and authority. With trauma parts, we comfort and lead them to Jesus. With evil alters, we confront the demonic contamination.

Process:

1. Bind any demonic interference.
2. Ask Jesus to separate the part from the demon.
3. Minister healing to the part once it is free.
4. Cast out the demon that tried to claim it.

This is delicate work. It requires discernment, humility, and Spirit-led authority. Always minister with covering and a team.

Ministry Process for Healing and Integration

So how do you walk someone through healing of fragmented parts and dissociation? Here is a general flow:

Step 1: Establish Safety

- Assure the person that all parts of them are welcome.
- Make the session environment safe, calm, and Spirit-filled.
- Invite Jesus to be present as Shepherd.

Step 2: Identify the Part

- When a part surfaces, ask: "Who am I speaking with?"

- The part may say, "I'm 8 years old," or "I'm the one who keeps us safe."
- Honor their identity without judgment.

Step 3: Hear the Story

- Allow the part to share why it exists.
- Ask what its job has been.
- Thank the part for protecting.

Step 4: Invite Jesus In

- Ask, "Jesus, would You come meet this part right now?"
- Let the part describe what it sees or senses.
- Encourage them to give their burden to Him.

Step 5: Healing and Release

- If the part is ready, lead them to forgive, release, and receive healing.
- If protectors resist, ask Jesus what they need to feel safe.
- With evil alters, separate the demonic and cast it out, then heal the part.

Step 6: Integration

- Ask, "Jesus, would You bring this part into wholeness with the rest of [name]?"
- Sometimes the part integrates right away—like a child running into the adult self.
- Sometimes Jesus keeps the part with Him until the person is ready. Both are valid.

Step 7: Seal the Work

- Pray for peace and protection over the soul.
- Remind the person that healing is a process. More parts may surface in time.
- Encourage continued community and discipleship.

Minister's Safeguards

Working with dissociation and fragmentation can be intense. Protect yourself and the ministry by:

- Always ministering with a helper present.
- Never pushing parts to speak more than they're ready.
- Staying accountable to leadership.
- Taking time for your own rest and healing.

Remember: you are not the healer. Jesus is. Your role is to host His presence, honor the parts, and trust Him to do the integration.

The Shepherd Restores the Soul

At the end of the day, this ministry is about Psalm 23: "He restores my soul." Fragmentation, dissociation, protectors, and evil alters are all evidence of how deeply trauma can wound. But they are also evidence of how powerfully Jesus can heal.

He gathers the fragments. He comforts the protectors. He separates the demonic. He integrates the soul. He brings wholeness where there was once only brokenness.

As a minister, you don't need to fear this work. You just

need to stay close to the Shepherd. He is faithful to restore every part.

Reflection Questions

1. HOW DOES MY UNDERSTANDING OF FRAGMENTATION AND dissociation shape the way I view people who carry deep trauma—and what attitudes, assumptions, or fears do I need Jesus to transform in me? When I imagine someone presenting with fragmented parts, do I internally respond with compassion, fear, confusion, or avoidance? Have I subconsciously judged or misunderstood dissociation in the past? What would it look like for me to fully see these individuals the way Jesus does—precious, courageous, and worthy of restoration?

2. AM I PREPARED TO HONOR PROTECTORS, DISCERN TRAUMA parts from demonic influence, and engage every part of the soul with both compassion and authority? How comfortable am I with the idea of protectors—angry, numb, or fearful parts that have been carrying impossible burdens? Does the idea of evil alters or demonic contamination make me anxious, overly aggressive, or hesitant? What strengths do I carry in discernment, and where do I need more equipping, covering, or inner healing to minister with clarity and peace?

3. HOW WILLING AM I TO FOLLOW JESUS' PACE IN THE LONG, SLOW work of fragmentation healing—and what expectations or pressures do I need to release as a minister? Do I feel pressure to "fix" someone, solve their fragmentation, or force integration before they're ready? How well do I handle slow progress, emotional intensity, or uncertainty in ministry? What would it look like for me to trust Jesus with the process, creating safety for every part without pushing, rushing, or overreaching?

10

RENOUNCING
UNHEALTHY SOUL TIES

THE BIBLE TEACHES THAT GOD DESIGNED US FOR CONNECTION. We are made to bond with Him and with others in love, trust, and covenant. But when those bonds are twisted through sin, abuse, or unhealthy dependence, they become chains instead of lifelines. These chains are what we call unhealthy soul ties.

Soul ties are real spiritual connections between people that join their souls together. In God's design, they are beautiful—like the bond between husband and wife, parent and child, brother and sister in Christ. But in the enemy's counterfeit, they can be destructive—tying people to shame, sin, fear, and oppression.

In this chapter, we'll look at what unhealthy soul ties are, how they form, the different kinds (sexual, emotional, occult, and codependent), and how to lead people in breaking them. I'll also give you prayers and declarations you can use in ministry to help people cut those ties and walk in freedom.

What Are Soul Ties?

A soul tie is a spiritual and emotional bond formed between two people. Scripture hints at this reality. First Samuel 18:1 says that "the soul of Jonathan was knit to the soul of David, and Jonathan loved him as his own soul." That's a healthy soul tie—a covenant friendship rooted in God.

But when souls are knit together outside God's order, the tie becomes unhealthy. Instead of bringing life, it brings bondage. Instead of freedom, it brings control.

Signs of unhealthy soul ties:

- Inability to move on from a past relationship.
- Feeling controlled or manipulated by someone even after separation.
- Persistent sexual or emotional pull toward someone from the past.
- Ongoing spiritual oppression tied to a person.
- Thoughts or emotions that feel "not my own," connected to someone else.

Sexual Soul Ties

One of the most powerful forms of soul ties is sexual. First Corinthians 6:16 says, *"Do you not know that he who is joined to a harlot is one body with her? For 'the two,' He says, 'shall become one flesh.'"* Sexual intimacy creates a bond—whether in marriage or outside of it.

When sexual intimacy happens outside of God's covenant of marriage, the soul tie becomes destructive. The person may carry shame, lust, or ongoing connection to every past partner.

As ministers, we must help people break these ties. It is not enough to repent of the act—they must also renounce the bond that was formed.

Prayer example:

"Lord, I repent for sexual sin with [name]. I renounce the soul tie created through that union. I cut it in Jesus' name. I declare that I am one spirit with You, Jesus, not with [name]."

Emotional Soul Ties

Not all soul ties are sexual. Many are emotional. These can form through unhealthy attachments, manipulative relationships, or co-dependent dynamics.

Examples:

- A controlling parent who keeps their adult child bound through guilt.
- A toxic friendship where one person dominates the other.
- A mentor or leader who uses spiritual authority to control.

These ties keep people trapped in fear or obligation. They often hear the other person's voice in their head, directing their choices.

Prayer example:

"Lord, I repent for unhealthy emotional attachment to [name]. I renounce the soul tie. I cut every controlling influence. I declare that I belong to You, and You alone define my worth."

Occult Soul Ties

Soul ties can also form through occult or covenantal practices. Witchcraft, blood covenants, or oaths bind people spiritually to others. In some cultures, blood brother rituals or occult initiations create lasting ties. These ties are demonic. They must be broken with authority.

Prayer example:

"Lord, I repent for every covenant I made with [person/group]. I renounce the blood tie, oath, or ritual. I cut it by the blood of Jesus. I declare every demonic bond broken and every spirit attached cast out."

Codependent Soul Ties

Codependency is when one person's identity and security are wrapped up in another. These ties may not be overtly abusive, but they are still unhealthy. They keep people from walking in freedom and dependence on God.

Example prayers:

"Lord, I repent for placing my identity in [name] instead of in You. I renounce the tie of codependency. I cut it in Jesus' name. I declare that my worth and security are in You alone."

Leading People to Break Ties and Restore Freedom

As a minister, here's how you can walk someone through breaking soul ties:

Step 1: Recognition

Help them identify the person or relationship. Ask:

- "Who comes to mind when you think of unhealthy influence in your life?"
- "Do you feel tied to anyone from your past that you can't move on from?"

Step 2: Repentance

Lead them to repent of any sin involved in forming the tie.

Step 3: Renunciation

Have them renounce the tie out loud, naming the person and the nature of the tie.

Step 4: Cutting the Tie

Lead them to declare:

"I cut every soul tie with [name] in the name of Jesus. I break its power and influence over me."

Some ministers use a symbolic action, like motioning with scissors or a sword of the Spirit. This can make the break more tangible.

Step 5: Replace with Truth

Ask Jesus to fill the place once occupied by the tie. Declare truth:

"I am one spirit with the Lord (1 Cor. 6:17). I belong fully to Him."

Prayers and Declarations for Cutting Ties

Here are some sample prayers you can use:

- Sexual ties: *"Lord, I repent for every sexual sin outside of marriage. I renounce every soul tie formed through sexual intimacy. I cut each tie by the blood of Jesus. I declare that I am washed, cleansed, and made new."*
- Emotional ties: *"Lord, I repent for unhealthy emotional attachment. I renounce manipulation and control. I cut the tie and declare that my emotions are healed and free in Christ."*
- Occult ties: *"Lord, I repent for every covenant, oath, or ritual I entered into. I renounce the occult bond. I cut it with the sword of the Spirit. I declare Jesus is my only covenant."*
- Codependent ties: *"Lord, I repent for making [name] my source of identity. I renounce the tie of codependency. I cut it and declare that I am secure in You alone."*

Minister's Role and Guardrails

As you lead people through this process:

- Stay Spirit-led. Don't assume ties—ask the Holy Spirit to reveal.
- Maintain dignity. Avoid shaming people as they confess past relationships.
- Be clear. Make sure they understand that renunciation is not just words but a decision of the will.
- Follow up. Encourage them to cut off ongoing contact if necessary.

Sometimes, after breaking ties, people experience immediate relief—like a weight lifting off. Other times, it takes repeated declaration and walking out the truth. Either way, freedom comes.

Belonging Fully to Jesus

Soul ties are the enemy's counterfeit for covenant. But the truth is this: we are meant to be tied—soul, spirit, and body—to Jesus. He is our covenant partner, our Bridegroom, our Lord. Every unhealthy tie must be cut so that we can belong fully to Him.

As ministers, our role is to lead people into repentance, renunciation, and declaration. We help them cut the cords that bind them to past sin, toxic people, or demonic covenants. We help them declare truth and walk in freedom.

When soul ties are broken, people feel it. They feel lighter, freer, whole. They realize they are no longer defined by their past—they are bound to Christ. And that is the bond that brings life.

Reflection Questions

1. WHAT RELATIONSHIPS FROM MY PAST OR PRESENT STILL EXERT influence over my emotions, decisions, identity, or sense of worth—and what does that reveal about possible unhealthy soul ties? Who comes to mind when you think of "influence that feels too strong or unhealthy"? Are there people you still feel tied to, even though the relationship is over or unhealthy? In what ways do those ties affect your freedom, peace, or ability to bond with God and others?

2. WHICH KINDS OF SOUL TIES—SEXUAL, EMOTIONAL, codependent, controlling, or occult—have influenced my life, and how have they shaped my identity, attachments, and spiritual walk? Have past sexual relationships, emotional entanglements, or controlling people shaped how you see yourself? Do you recognize any ties formed through guilt, fear, manipulation, or unmet needs? How have these ties impacted your relationships, boundaries, or ability to move on?

3. WHAT RESISTANCE DO I FEEL TOWARD BREAKING SOUL TIES— and what truth is Jesus inviting me to receive in place of those old bonds? Do you feel hesitation, fear, shame, or loyalty when you think about breaking a tie? What lies are attached to that tie (e.g., "I owe them," "I need them," "I can't be free," "This is who I am")? What truth does Jesus want to establish in place of that tie—and what would your life look like fully bonded to Him instead?

11

RITUAL ABUSE AND DARK TRAUMA

FEW AREAS OF MINISTRY REQUIRE AS MUCH DISCERNMENT, compassion, and courage as ministering to those who have endured ritual abuse or dark trauma. These individuals often carry wounds so deep, so hidden, and so overwhelming that many ministers shy away. But Jesus is not afraid of darkness. He came to destroy the works of the devil (1 John 3:8), and that includes the most sinister forms of bondage.

Ritual abuse refers to trauma inflicted through organized, intentional acts of cruelty—often with demonic or occult intent. Survivors may come from satanic ritual abuse (SRA) backgrounds, cults, generational occult families, or even abusive groups masquerading as religious. This trauma is usually repeated, severe, and paired with deliberate indoctrination, oaths, or covenants meant to enslave the person to darkness.

As ministers of healing, we need to know how to recognize survivors of ritual abuse, how to walk with them safely, and how to help them break free from vows, covenants, and lies. At the same time, we must understand our boundaries: some cases require legal or medical intervention, and we must remain wise, accountable, and Spirit-led.

What Ritual Abuse Is and How to Recognize It

Ritual abuse goes beyond ordinary trauma. It is systematic and usually connected to cultic or occult practices. Survivors are often subjected to:

- Sexual violation.
- Torture or extreme pain.
- Forced participation in rituals.
- Involvement in animal or human sacrifice (whether real or staged).
- Being made to witness horrifying events.
- Binding covenants through blood, vows, or oaths.

The goal is to fracture the soul, instill terror, and bind the person through demonic agreement. Survivors are often programmed to remain silent, to distrust outsiders, and to believe they can never escape.

As a minister, you may not hear the words "ritual abuse" right away. Survivors often use vague language: "dark stuff happened," "I was in something I can't talk about," or "I have nightmares I don't understand." Sometimes they won't remember at all, but fragments or flashbacks surface in ministry.

Red flags can include:

- Intense fear of religious settings.
- Unexplained physical symptoms during prayer (shaking, burning sensations, pain).

- Strong demonic manifestations when God's presence increases.
- Sudden switches in personality or voice (due to dissociation and programming).
- Memories or flashbacks of rituals, symbols, or oaths.

Not every case of trauma is ritual abuse. But when multiple red flags are present, you need to proceed with extra sensitivity and discernment.

Red Flags: Trauma Presentation, Dissociation, Flashbacks

Survivors of ritual abuse often carry complex trauma. Here's what you may observe:

- Dissociation. Many survivors develop Dissociative Identity Disorder (DID) as a survival mechanism. Different parts of the personality carry different memories, often created intentionally through trauma.
- Flashbacks. Survivors may suddenly relive events with vivid detail—sights, sounds, smells. Their body may react as if the trauma is happening now.
- Phobias and triggers. Specific words, images, or even Bible verses may trigger terror.
- Protectors. Some parts of the person may threaten, mock, or resist ministry—these were trained by abusers to keep the system intact.
- Shame and secrecy. Survivors may feel deep shame, convinced the abuse was their fault.

As a minister, your posture must be calm, grounded, and trauma-informed. When flashbacks happen, help the person ground themselves:

- "You're safe right now. It's [year]. You're here with me."
- "Take a deep breath. Feel your feet on the floor."
- "Jesus, cover this memory in Your light."

Never push for details. Survivors may not even remember everything accurately. Your job is not to investigate but to host healing.

Safe Protocols: Legal/Medical Considerations

This kind of ministry demands wisdom. Here are non-negotiables:

- Never promise secrecy. Tell the person from the start: "I will keep what you share confidential, except if you reveal someone is in current danger (especially a child). Then I am legally and morally bound to report."
- Know your laws. In many countries and states, ministers are mandated reporters for child abuse. Ignoring this could put you and others at risk.
- Don't play detective. Your role is not to verify memories or investigate perpetrators. Leave that to professionals. Your role is to bring Jesus into pain.
- Encourage professional support. Many survivors benefit from trauma-informed counseling or medical care alongside ministry. Don't shame them for needing it.
- Minister with accountability. Never meet alone with survivors of ritual abuse. Always have another trusted minister present.

This doesn't mean you can't minister powerfully—it means

you stay in your lane. You're not called to solve crimes. You're called to bind up the brokenhearted and set captives free.

Breaking Ritual Vows and Covenants

One of the defining features of ritual abuse is forced covenants. Survivors are often made to speak vows like:

- "I belong to Satan."
- "I will never tell."
- "I am cursed forever."

These vows create real spiritual bondage. They must be broken through repentance, renunciation, and declaration.
Steps for ministry:

1. Recognition: Help the survivor identify any vows or oaths they remember. If they can't remember specifics, ask Jesus to reveal what needs to be broken.
2. Repentance: Lead them in repenting for any agreements made—even if forced. "*Lord, I repent for every vow I was made to speak.*"
3. Renunciation: Have them declare: "*In the name of Jesus, I renounce every covenant, oath, or vow I made in rituals. I break agreement with them.*"
4. Declaration of belonging: Lead them to proclaim: "*I declare that I belong to Jesus Christ alone. He bought me with His blood. I am His.*"

Symbolic acts can be powerful here. Sometimes tearing up paper (representing contracts), cutting ropes, or declaring with raised hands: "Every covenant with darkness is broken!" reinforces the reality of freedom.

Restoring Identity in Christ

Ritual abuse is designed to destroy identity. Survivors are told they are worthless, cursed, evil, or unredeemable. Some are even given new names in rituals, stripping them of their God-given identity. Your role as a minister is to anchor them in truth:

- They are chosen. (Eph. 1:4)
- They are beloved. (1 John 3:1)
- They are redeemed. (Eph. 1:7)
- They are seated with Christ. (Eph. 2:6)
- They are new creations. (2 Cor. 5:17)

You may want to lead them through a renaming process:

"Jesus, what name do You call them? What do You say over their life?"

Hearing Jesus speak identity often undoes years of lies. Some survivors receive a Scripture, some a prophetic image, some a simple phrase like, "You are Mine." This is not fluff—it is warfare. Identity breaks chains.

Practical Ministering Flow

Here's an example of how a session might look:

1. Prayer of safety. "Jesus, cover this room in Your blood. Surround us with angels."
2. Grounding. Help the survivor feel present and safe.
3. Invite Jesus. "Lord, would You enter this memory, this flashback, this fear?"

4. Expose vows. "Jesus, are there any vows or covenants that need to be broken today?"
5. Lead repentance/renunciation. Help the person repent and break agreement.
6. Declare identity. Lead them to proclaim who they are in Christ.
7. Close in peace. Ask Jesus to seal the work and bring rest.

Minister's Boundaries

A final word of caution: this ministry is heavy. Survivors of ritual abuse often require years of healing. You are not their savior. Don't take on a "messiah complex." Stay in accountability. Know when to refer. Keep your own rhythms of rest and joy.

The enemy would love to use ritual abuse ministry to burn you out or isolate you. Don't let him. Stay in community. Stay humble. Stay submitted.

Light Overcomes Darkness

John 1:5 ESV says, "*The light shines in the darkness, and the darkness has not overcome it.*" That is the banner over ritual abuse ministry.

Yes, the trauma is dark. Yes, the stories are horrifying. But the light of Jesus is greater. His blood breaks every vow. His presence heals every fragment. His truth restores every shattered identity.

You don't need to be afraid of ritual abuse. You need to be grounded, wise, and Spirit-led. If you stay rooted in Jesus, the darkness has no chance. He is the Deliverer. He is the Healer.

And He is the One who restores survivors of ritual abuse into radiant sons and daughters of God.

Reflection Questions

1. HOW PREPARED IS MY HEART, THEOLOGY, AND EMOTIONAL capacity to minister to survivors of ritual abuse? What emotions rise in you when you think about ministering in cases of ritual abuse? Have you ever held misconceptions such as "this is too dark," "this is beyond help," or "I'm not equipped,"? How might Jesus want to correct those views? What foundational truths about Jesus' authority, deliverance, and identity do you need to anchor yourself in before entering this kind of ministry?

2. WHAT BOUNDARIES, SAFEGUARDS, AND ACCOUNTABILITY structures do I personally have in place—and where might I still be vulnerable to burnout, overreach, or stepping outside my lane? Do you have clear lines between your role (minister) and the roles of mental health professionals, law enforcement, or medical personnel? How strong is your current support system? Where might you be tempted to overextend, rescue, or isolate yourself when ministering to high-trauma cases?

3. HOW WELL DO I CARRY THE HEART OF JESUS WHEN ENGAGING dissociation, protectors, ritual vows, or demonic contamination? When faced with protectors, switches, or fear-driven reactions, do I instinctively respond with compassion or with frustration, pressure, or fear? Can I differentiate between trauma parts needing comfort and demonic elements needing authority? Do I depend on the Spirit rather than assumptions? What qualities of Jesus do I want Him to form more deeply in me as I minister to severe trauma?

12

HEALING GRIEF AND LOSS

EVERY PERSON WHO WALKS THIS EARTH WILL FACE LOSS. IT IS PART of the human journey in a fallen world. We lose people we love. We lose dreams we carried. We lose seasons we hoped would last forever. Grief is unavoidable, but it is not unredeemable. In fact, grief can become one of the most powerful doorways to encounter Jesus as Healer and Comforter.

The challenge is that most people don't know how to grieve. They either stuff it down, deny it, or get stuck in it. Some confuse trauma with grief. Others believe faith means they should smile through the pain and pretend everything is fine. But the Bible shows us a different way: lament. Lament is the language of grief turned into prayer. It is how the people of God have always brought their sorrow before Him.

In this chapter, we'll look at the difference between trauma and grief, the gift of biblical lament, how to walk through specific losses like death, miscarriage, betrayal, and lost dreams, and finally how God brings us from sorrow into joy.

The Difference Between Trauma and Grief

It's important to distinguish between trauma and grief. Trauma is a wound—an overwhelming experience that shatters safety and leaves a scar in the soul. Grief, on the other hand, is the natural process of mourning what was lost.

- Trauma says, "I'm not safe. I can't cope."
- Grief says, "I've lost something or someone I love."

Of course, the two often overlap. The death of a loved one may carry trauma if it was sudden, violent, or unexpected. Miscarriage can feel traumatic as well as deeply sorrowful. Betrayal can bring trauma to the heart and grief to the soul.

As ministers, we must discern: Is this person primarily dealing with trauma, grief, or both? Trauma often requires revisiting the wound with Jesus to bring healing. Grief requires walking with Jesus through the valley of sorrow until joy dawns again.

Biblical Lament as Part of Healing

The Bible is not silent about grief. In fact, it is full of it. Job grieved his losses. David poured out laments in the Psalms. Jeremiah wrote an entire book called Lamentations. Even Jesus wept at the tomb of Lazarus (John 11:35).

Lament is not unbelief. Lament is worship in pain. It is choosing to bring your sorrow to God instead of turning away.

The pattern of lament in Scripture looks like this:

1. Turn to God. Instead of running from Him, bring your pain directly to Him.
2. Pour out your complaint. Be honest about the loss, the anger, the questions.
3. Ask boldly for help. Invite God into the pain.
4. Choose to trust. Re-anchor in who He is, even when the loss remains.

Psalm 13 is a perfect example:

- "How long, O Lord? Will You forget me forever?" (complaint)
- "Consider and hear me, O Lord my God." (request)
- "But I have trusted in Your mercy; my heart shall rejoice in Your salvation." (trust)

Teaching people to lament frees them from stuffing grief or drowning in it. It gives them a Spirit-led way to move through loss.

Healing the Pain of Death

Death is the most final of losses in this life. It leaves an empty seat at the table, an ache in the heart, and a silence that feels deafening.

As ministers, we must give people permission to grieve deeply. Too often Christians are told, "Don't cry, they're in heaven." But tears are not a sign of unbelief. Tears are a sign of love. Jesus Himself wept at Lazarus' tomb, even though He knew He was about to raise him.

How to minister in grief from death:

- Honor the loss. Say their name. Acknowledge the hole left behind.
- Invite Jesus into the grief. "Lord, where are You in this pain?"
- Address lies. Many blame themselves or God. Help them hear His truth.
- Guide lament. Lead them to pour out sorrow and then choose trust.
- Bless remembrance. Encourage them to celebrate the life, not erase it.

Death may always carry sadness, but Jesus promises joy will come in the morning (Psalm 30:5).

Healing the Pain of Miscarriage

Miscarriage is often overlooked grief. Many minimize it: "It was early." But to the mother and father, it was a child. The loss is real.

For mothers, miscarriage can bring shame ("What's wrong with me?"), guilt ("Did I cause this?"), or anger at God. For fathers, it often brings silent grief, unacknowledged by others.
As ministers:

- Acknowledge the child. Encourage parents to name the baby if they desire.
- Give permission to grieve. Validate their loss.
- Release guilt. Lead them to renounce false responsibility.
- Invite Jesus into the memory. Ask Him to show where the child is now—in His presence, safe and whole.

Helping parents see their child with Jesus often brings profound comfort.

Healing the Pain of Betrayal

Betrayal is a unique kind of grief. It's not just about losing a relationship—it's about losing trust. A spouse who cheats, a friend who betrays, a leader who abuses authority—these losses cut to the core.

Betrayal carries layers: grief over the relationship, trauma of deception, and bitterness that clings.

As ministers:

- Name the betrayal. Don't sugarcoat it.
- Lead them into forgiveness. Not excusing, but releasing.
- Address inner vows. ("I'll never trust again.")
- Invite Jesus into the wound. Let Him speak truth.
- Restore trust in God first. Rebuild slowly with others.

Healing from betrayal is often slow, but with Jesus, hearts can learn to trust again.

Healing the Pain of Lost Dreams

Not all grief is about people. Some grief is about the loss of what could have been. The dream that died. The career that never worked out. The ministry that collapsed. The marriage that never happened.

These losses can feel less visible, but they still wound deeply. Proverbs 13:12 says,

"Hope deferred makes the heart sick."

As ministers:

- Validate the grief. Don't dismiss it.
- Help them surrender. Lead them to give the dream to Jesus.
- Ask Jesus for His perspective. Sometimes He gives a new dream. Sometimes He resurrects the old one. Sometimes He simply gives peace.
- Point to His faithfulness. Remind them He redeems all things.

Lost dreams can become seeds that produce new life when surrendered to God.

Moving from Sorrow to Joy

Grief is a valley, not a destination. God does not ask us to deny sorrow, but He promises to lead us through it. Psalm 84:6 says of those who walk through the Valley of Baca (valley of weeping), that they make it a place of springs.

The journey of grief looks like this:

1. Acknowledgment. Naming the loss honestly.
2. Lament. Bringing it to God in prayer.
3. Release. Forgiving, surrendering, letting go.
4. Renewal. Receiving His comfort and new life.
5. Joy. Emerging with peace and hope restored.

Joy is not the absence of sorrow. It is the presence of Jesus in the midst of it. Over time, His joy outweighs the sorrow.

Practical Ministry Tools

- Grief journaling. Encourage writing letters to God about the loss.
- Empty chair. Picture the lost person or dream, say what needs to be said, then release them to Jesus.
- Scripture anchors. Psalm 34:18, Matthew 5:4, Revelation 21:4.
- Symbolic acts. Lighting a candle, planting a tree, releasing balloons—physical acts that honor and release.
- Prayer of exchange. "Jesus, I give You my sorrow. What do You want to give me in return?"

Minister's Posture

When ministering to grief:

- Be patient. Don't rush the process.
- Be present. Sometimes silence and tears together are the ministry.
- Avoid clichés. "They're in a better place" often wounds more than it heals.
- Point to Jesus. He alone carries sorrow and brings joy.

The God Who Turns Mourning into Dancing

Psalm 30:11 says,

"You have turned for me my mourning into dancing; You have put off my sackcloth and clothed me with gladness."

That is the testimony of every believer who brings their grief to Jesus.

Grief is real. Loss is painful. But the story doesn't end there. With Jesus, sorrow gives way to joy, mourning to dancing, despair to hope. As ministers, we have the privilege of walking with people through the valley of loss into the light of resurrection life.

Reflection Questions

1. WHEN LOSS ENTERS MY LIFE, WHAT DO I INSTINCTIVELY DO AND what does that reveal about how I understand Him, myself, and grief? Do I believe expressing grief is weakness? Do I use faith to avoid feeling pain? Do I collapse into it and get stuck? Do I attempt to "be strong" instead of being honest? What does my response reveal about what I believe God is like in my pain?

2. WHICH LOSS IN MY LIFE—RECENT OR LONG BURIED—HAS never fully been acknowledged, grieved, or lamented, and what invitation might Jesus be extending for me to revisit that place with Him now? This helps uncover unprocessed grief, whether from: Childhood losses, Broken relationships, Miscarriage or infertility, Missed opportunities, Death of a dream, Past betrayals.

3. HOW COMFORTABLE AM I WITH BIBLICAL LAMENT—AND WHAT would it look like for me to practice lament as an act of worship, rather than avoid grief out of fear, shame, or false strength? Have I equated lament with unbelief? Have I ever prayed a Psalm-like lament honestly? Do I allow myself to feel what God already knows I feel? What changes when I treat lament not as emotional failure but as sacred connection to God?

PART III

TOOLS AND PRACTICES

13

THE WORD OF GOD IN HEALING

WHEN EVERYTHING ELSE SHAKES, THE WORD OF GOD REMAINS. Heaven and earth will pass away, but His Word will never pass away (Matt. 24:35). If we want to see lasting inner healing, it cannot rest only on an encounter, an emotion, or even a break-through moment. Those things are beautiful, but they must be anchored in the unchanging truth of Scripture.

When people are wounded, they often believe lies about themselves, about God, or about others. The only thing strong enough to uproot a lie is truth. And not just any truth, but God's truth revealed in His Word. As inner healing ministers, we are not just walking people through memories and emotions—we are equipping them to fight for their freedom with the Word of God.

This chapter will unpack how Scripture anchors identity, comfort, and truth. We'll also look at how to teach people to fight lies with the Word, both in ministry sessions and in their daily lives.

The Word Anchors Identity

At the root of most wounds is a distortion of identity. Abuse whispers, "You are worthless." Abandonment whispers, "You are unlovable." Failure whispers, "You are a disappointment." These lies take root in the soul and shape how people see themselves. But the Word of God speaks a better identity.

- "You are fearfully and wonderfully made." (Psalm 139:14)
- "You are chosen in Him before the foundation of the world." (Eph. 1:4)
- "You are a new creation in Christ." (2 Cor. 5:17)
- "You are God's workmanship, created for good works." (Eph. 2:10)
- "You are seated with Christ in heavenly places." (Eph. 2:6)

When someone is battling shame, guilt, or self-hatred, you must lead them to these truths. Don't just quote verses at them —help them encounter the living Word. Have them read it out loud. Have them put their name in the verse. Have them declare it until it sinks in.

Example: Instead of just saying, "You are chosen," have them declare: "I, Tom, am chosen in Christ before the foundation of the world." Identity becomes real when it is spoken and received.

The Word Brings Comfort

Grief, trauma, and loss leave people raw. In those moments, the comfort of Scripture is like water to a parched soul. The

Psalms are especially powerful here—they give language to pain while anchoring trust in God.

- "The Lord is near to the brokenhearted and saves the crushed in spirit." (Psalm 34:18)
- "Even though I walk through the valley of the shadow of death, I will fear no evil, for You are with me." (Psalm 23:4)
- "Those who sow in tears shall reap with shouts of joy." (Psalm 126:5)
- "Blessed are those who mourn, for they shall be comforted." (Matt. 5:4)

Sometimes the most healing thing you can do is open the Bible and let the person sit in the Word. Have them close their eyes and listen to Psalm 23 read slowly. Have them breathe deeply while you pray Psalm 46 over them:

"God is our refuge and strength, a very present help in trouble."

The Word doesn't just inform; it comforts. It reassures the soul that God is still present, still faithful, still loving.

The Word Confronts Lies

The devil is the father of lies (John 8:44). Every wound he exploits comes with a lie attached. The only way to break the lie is with truth, and truth is found in the Word.

When Jesus was tempted in the wilderness, He didn't argue with the devil or explain Himself. He said, "It is written." (Matt. 4:4, 7, 10). That is the model for us.

Common lies people believe and the Word that breaks them:

- Lie: "I am dirty because of what happened to me."
- Truth: "Though your sins are like scarlet, they shall be as white as snow." (Isa. 1:18)
- Lie: "I will always be alone."
- Truth: "I will never leave you nor forsake you." (Heb. 13:5)
- Lie: "I'm powerless and hopeless."
- Truth: "I can do all things through Christ who strengthens me." (Phil. 4:13)
- Lie: "God doesn't love me."
- Truth: "Nothing can separate us from the love of God in Christ Jesus our Lord." (Rom. 8:39)
- Lie: "My past defines me."
- Truth: "If anyone is in Christ, he is a new creation. Old things have passed away; all things have become new." (2 Cor. 5:17)

Help people replace lies with truth. Write down the lies on one side of a paper, then write God's truth on the other. Have them physically cross out the lie and declare the truth out loud.

Teaching People to Fight with the Word

Deliverance and inner healing sessions are powerful, but the real battle often comes later. When the enemy tries to whisper lies again, the person must know how to fight with the Word themselves.

Equip them to:

1. Identify the lie. "What am I hearing or feeling that doesn't line up with God's Word?"
2. Find the truth. "What does the Bible say about this?"
3. Speak it out. "It is written..." Speak it until the atmosphere shifts.

4. Stand on it. Don't just use it once. Keep declaring it until the lie loses power.

Encourage them to build a personal arsenal of Scriptures. I often tell people: "You need verses in your mouth, not just in your Bible."

Scriptures for Healing and Identity

Here is a list you can use in ministry and encourage people to memorize:

- Identity: John 1:12, Romans 8:15–17, 1 Peter 2:9.
- Comfort: Psalm 23, Psalm 91, 2 Cor. 1:3–4.
- Freedom: John 8:32, Galatians 5:1, Colossians 1:13.
- Renewal: Romans 12:2, Ephesians 4:22–24.
- Strength: Isaiah 40:31, Philippians 4:13.

You can build prayer and declaration exercises around these verses. For example:

"I am not a slave to fear. I am a child of God (Rom. 8:15). I am chosen, holy, and loved (Col. 3:12). God has delivered me from the domain of darkness (Col. 1:13)."

Minister's Role in the Word

Your job as a minister is not just to comfort or counsel, but to equip. Don't just use Scripture in the session—teach the person how to wield it themselves. Give them "homework." Ask them to memorize one verse and declare it daily. Encourage them to journal lies they hear and then write the truth next to them.

When you do this, you're not just helping them heal—you're discipling them into maturity. Healing is not only about relief; it's about equipping people to live in ongoing freedom.

The Word That Heals

Hebrews 4:12 says, *"For the Word of God is living and powerful, and sharper than any two-edged sword, piercing even to the division of soul and spirit, and of joints and marrow, and is a discerner of the thoughts and intents of the heart."*

That is exactly what happens in inner healing. The Word pierces the lies, discerns the heart, and brings division between what is soulish and what is Spirit. It cuts away what doesn't belong and establishes what does.

As a minister, you must keep the Word central. It is not an optional add-on; it is the foundation. When you anchor identity, comfort, and truth in Scripture, you are building on rock, not sand. And when the storms come, those who have built their healing on the Word will stand.

Reflection Questions

1. WHEN LIES SURFACE IN MY OWN LIFE—ABOUT MY WORTH, MY identity, or God's character—what do I instinctively reach for first: my feelings, others' opinions, or the Word of God? What does that reveal about where my heart truly places authority? Do I treat Scripture as final truth or optional encouragement? Do my emotions govern my beliefs more than the Word? How does my instinctive response to lies reveal my spiritual formation?

2. WHICH SCRIPTURES HAVE MOST SHAPED MY IDENTITY—AND where are there still gaps where I am vulnerable to attack because I have not yet armed myself with God's truth? Which identity Scriptures do I actually *know* versus vaguely *agree with*? Where do I still struggle with shame, rejection, unworthiness, or fear? What truths has God spoken that I have not yet fully internalized?

3. HOW ACTIVELY DO I FIGHT SPIRITUAL LIES—BOTH FOR MYSELF and others—using the Word? Do I wield Scripture like a sword, or do I lean mostly on emotion, willpower, and experiences when battling deception? Do I have a habit of declaring Scripture out loud? Do I know how to confront lies with the truth the way Jesus did—"It is written"? How can I grow in using the Word not just as information, but as a weapon, a shield, and an anchor in inner healing ministry?

14

THE ROLE OF PRAYER AND PROPHETIC MINISTRY

AT THE HEART OF ALL INNER HEALING IS THE PRESENCE OF GOD. We don't heal by clever techniques or counseling skills. Healing comes when Jesus shows up and speaks into the broken places. And the primary way we make space for that is through prayer and prophetic ministry.

Prayer is not just words—it is communion with the Father. Prophetic ministry is not just predictions—it is hearing God's heart and speaking it into wounds. Together, prayer and prophecy create the atmosphere where lies are replaced with truth, shame is broken, and the brokenhearted encounter the living God.

This chapter will explore the role of prayer in healing, different kinds of prayers we use in sessions, and how prophetic encouragement and renaming wounded places becomes a powerful tool for restoration.

Listening Prayer

One of the most important practices in inner healing is listening prayer. Instead of rushing to fill the silence with our own words, we pause and ask: "Jesus, what do You want to say here?"

Listening prayer acknowledges that the Holy Spirit is the true Counselor. He knows the wound, the lie, and the truth that sets free. When we invite the person to listen for themselves, it empowers them to hear God directly.

How to use listening prayer in sessions:

- When a wound surfaces, pause and ask: "Jesus, where were You in that memory?"
- When a lie is exposed, ask: "Jesus, what is Your truth about this?"
- When forgiveness feels impossible, ask: "Jesus, show them how You see the person who hurt them."
- When the person feels shame, ask: "Jesus, what do You say about who they are?"

Listening prayer turns ministry from a conversation between minister and person into an encounter between person and God. And that's where real transformation happens.

Blessing Prayers

Another powerful form of prayer in healing is blessing. Too often, wounded people have lived under cursing words: "You're worthless." "You'll never change." "You're just like your father." These curses become scripts that play over and over in their minds.

Blessing prayers do the opposite. They speak God's heart,

God's truth, and God's favor over the person. Proverbs 18:21 says, "Death and life are in the power of the tongue." When you bless, you release life.

Examples of blessing prayers:

- "I bless you to know you are deeply loved by the Father."
- "I bless you with courage to walk in freedom."
- "I bless you to rest in God's peace and not strive for love."
- "I bless your identity as a son/daughter of God."
- "I bless your emotions to be safe, healed, and whole."

Blessing prayers can be Spirit-led or drawn directly from Scripture. They not only break curses but plant seeds of truth in the heart.

Prophetic Encouragement

Paul tells us in 1 Corinthians 14:3 that prophecy is for "edification, exhortation, and comfort." That is exactly what wounded hearts need. Prophetic encouragement is not about predicting the future—it is about speaking God's now-word into places of pain.

Prophetic encouragement looks like:

- Speaking destiny. "I see God's call on your life as a restorer of others."
- Calling out identity. "You are not abandoned; you are chosen."
- Affirming God's presence. "I sense the Lord saying He has always been with you, even when you felt alone."

- Renaming. "You've been called worthless, but God calls you precious."

Prophetic ministry breaks the narrative of lies and rewrites the script with God's perspective. When people hear God's voice in their pain, it changes everything.

Renaming Wounded Places

All through Scripture, God renames people as part of their healing and destiny. Abram became Abraham. Sarai became Sarah. Jacob became Israel. Simon became Peter. Saul became Paul. Names carry identity.

Wounded people often carry false names in their hearts: "Failure." "Rejected." "Unwanted." Prophetic ministry has the power to rename those places with God's truth.

Practical process for renaming:

1. Identify the false name. Ask: "What do you feel this wound has named you?"
2. (Examples: "Worthless," "Dirty," "Weak.")
3. Ask Jesus: "What name do You give instead?"
4. Listen. Sometimes He gives a Scripture, sometimes a word, sometimes an image.
5. Declare it. Have the person speak out: "I reject the name 'Worthless.' I receive the name 'Beloved.'"

This is not symbolic only—it is spiritual. Names are powerful. When people embrace their God-given name, the wound loses authority.

Minister's Posture in Prayer and Prophecy

As ministers, we must keep these guardrails:

- Stay Spirit-dependent. Don't make up encouraging words—wait for the Spirit.
- Keep it biblical. Prophetic words must align with Scripture.
- Stay humble. Present words as encouragement, not commands. "I sense..." not "Thus says the Lord."
- Protect safety. Never use prophecy to control or manipulate. Always keep ministry in integrity.

When done rightly, prayer and prophetic ministry bring healing faster than anything else because they bypass human reasoning and let God speak directly.

Practical Exercises

Here are some tools you can use:

- Listening Exercise: After identifying a wound, have the person close their eyes and ask Jesus one simple question: "What do You want me to know about this?" Wait in silence. Then process what they hear.
- Blessing Declaration: Write out a list of biblical blessings (identity, freedom, peace). Speak them over the person at the end of the session.
- Prophetic Renaming: Ask Jesus, "What do You call me in this place?" Have the person write it down, declare it, and keep it as a reminder.
- Prophetic Journaling: Encourage people to journal with God daily, asking Him questions and writing down what they sense.

Prayer and Prophecy as Healing Streams

Inner healing is not about formulas. It is about presence—the presence of God. Prayer opens the conversation. Prophecy delivers His heart. Together, they create streams of healing.

Isaiah 55:11 says God's Word does not return void but accomplishes what He sends it to do. When we pray and prophesy in His Spirit, healing happens. Wounded hearts receive comfort. Lies are replaced with truth. Old names are exchanged for new ones. And people walk away not just with relief, but with a living word from God that anchors them in freedom.

As an inner healing minister, make prayer and prophetic encouragement central. Don't rush past them. Give space for Jesus to speak. Bless lavishly. Prophesy encouragement. Help people receive new names.

This is the ministry of Jesus. He still speaks. He still heals. And He has called us to carry His voice into the broken places of the world.

Reflection Questions

1. In my ministry, do I tend to rely more on my own words, insight, or techniques—or on creating space for Jesus to speak directly through listening prayer? What does this reveal about my trust in the Holy Spirit as the true Counselor? Do I get uncomfortable with silence? Do I feel pressure to "fix" people with my own wisdom? How often do I pause and ask, "Jesus, what do You want to say right now?"

2. What false names or labels have shaped me or the people I minister to, and how has prophetic encouragement or renaming shifted those identities toward God's truth? What names—"Rejected," "Unworthy," "Failure," "Too Much," "Invisible"—have operated in my own life? How do I respond when Jesus reveals a new name over a wounded place? How might renaming be a key part of the healing God wants to do through me?

3. How do I currently approach prophetic ministry—do I use it to edify, comfort, and build up (1 Cor. 14:3), or do I hesitate out of fear, insecurity, or misunderstanding? What would it look like to grow in safe, humble, Scripture-anchored prophetic encouragement? Am I bold enough to speak God's heart when He nudges me? Do I avoid prophecy because I fear being wrong or overstepping? How can I better steward encouragement and identity-shaping words? What safeguards and humility do I practice?

15

WORSHIP AND THE PRESENCE OF GOD

IF THERE IS ONE THING THAT CONSISTENTLY SHIFTS ATMOSPHERES, heals hearts, and restores hope, it is worship. Worship is not just the singing of songs—it is the posture of the heart that exalts God above everything else. Worship takes our eyes off the pain, the trauma, the loss, and the lies, and it fixes them on Jesus, the Healer of our souls.

In inner healing ministry, worship is not an optional add-on. It is central. It sets the atmosphere for encounters. It tenderizes hearts. It silences the enemy. It ushers in the presence of God, and His presence is where transformation happens. You can have the best tools and training in the world, but if the presence of God is not there, no lasting healing will come. But when His presence fills the room, things shift in a moment.

In this chapter, I want to share why worship is vital in healing, how it sets an atmosphere for God's power, and how we can lead people into encounters with His love through worship.

Worship as Atmosphere for Healing

The Bible is full of examples of worship creating an atmosphere where God moves.

- In 2 Chronicles 20, Jehoshaphat sent singers ahead of the army, and as they worshiped, God set ambushes against their enemies. Worship shifted the battle.
- In Acts 16, Paul and Silas sang hymns in prison. As they worshiped, an earthquake shook the foundations, doors opened, and chains fell off. Worship shifted the atmosphere.
- In 1 Samuel 16, David played the harp, and the tormenting spirit left Saul. Worship brought deliverance.

Worship doesn't just prepare us for ministry—it is ministry. It shifts atmospheres both in the spirit realm and in the human heart. When people come into a session carrying fear, shame, or heaviness, worship can break that off before a single word of counsel is given.

Practical steps:

- Begin sessions with a few moments of worship—soft music, singing, or simply exalting God with spoken praise.
- Encourage the person to focus on Jesus rather than the problem.
- Remind them that healing flows from His presence, not from striving.

Worship Breaks Chains

Why is worship so powerful? Because worship enthrones

God. Psalm 22:3 says God inhabits the praises of His people. When God is enthroned, every other power must bow.

Demons cannot stay where Jesus is exalted. Lies cannot stand in the face of truth declared in worship. Fear loses power when love is magnified. Worship literally changes the spiritual climate.

Many times in deliverance and healing ministry, I have seen breakthrough come not from direct confrontation but from worship. When the room shifts into adoration of Jesus, demons get restless. They know the King has entered. Sometimes the most effective warfare is not shouting at the darkness but lifting up the Light.

Worship Heals the Heart

Worship is not only warfare—it is intimacy. When people are wounded, they need more than deliverance from the enemy; they need an encounter with the love of God. Worship creates a space where that encounter happens. When we worship, we experience:

- God's love. Romans 5:5 says His love is poured out in our hearts through the Holy Spirit. Worship opens us to receive that love.
- God's peace. Isaiah 26:3 promises perfect peace to those whose minds are stayed on Him. Worship fixes our minds on Him.
- God's joy. In His presence is fullness of joy (Psalm 16:11). Worship brings us into that presence.

I have seen people break down in tears of healing during worship before we even begin ministry. Why? Because worship bypasses the defenses of the mind and reaches the heart. It opens the soul to the reality of God's goodness.

Leading People into Encounters with God's Love

As ministers, our role is to lead people beyond songs into encounters. Worship is not just about music—it's about opening the door to God's presence. Here are some practical ways:

1. Create space for stillness.

Don't rush. Sometimes healing happens in silence as soft worship plays and people wait on the Lord. Stillness helps them hear His voice.

2. Invite Jesus by name.

Encourage people to picture Jesus with them as they worship. Ask: "Where is He in the room right now? What is He doing?"

3. Use Scripture in worship.

Sing or declare Scriptures. Psalm 103, Psalm 91, and Revelation 4–5 are powerful passages to magnify Jesus.

4. Guide the person's focus.

If they are stuck in fear or shame, gently redirect: "Let's lift our eyes to Jesus together. Let's thank Him for His faithfulness."

5. Release prophetic worship.

Sometimes spontaneous songs or words of love to Jesus break open encounters. Encourage freedom in the Spirit.

Testimonies of Healing in Worship

I've seen people healed of trauma just by resting in worship. One woman, abused as a child, began to cry as we sang "Jesus loves me." She said she suddenly saw Jesus sitting with her as a child, singing that song over her. Years of pain began to unravel in a single encounter.

Another time, a man tormented by fear for years fell to his knees in worship and began laughing uncontrollably in the joy of the Lord. He said it felt like fear left him as joy filled him. No one had to cast anything out—worship shifted the atmosphere.

Minister's Posture in Worship

As ministers, we must be worshipers first. We cannot lead people where we have not gone. Carry a personal altar of worship in your life. Let your secret place be full of songs and adoration. Out of that overflow, you will bring others into His presence. In sessions:

- Don't use worship as filler—use it as an intentional tool.
- Stay sensitive to the Spirit. Sometimes two minutes is enough. Sometimes thirty minutes are needed.
- Never make it about performance. Worship is not a concert. It's an encounter.

Practical Tools

- Playlist of healing worship songs. Prepare a set of songs that focus on God's love, peace, and presence.
- Live worship if possible. If you have a team, bring in worshipers to set the atmosphere.
- Encourage personal worship. Teach those you minister to make worship a lifestyle, not just a session practice.
- Use instruments or spontaneous praise. A guitar, a piano, or even acapella singing can shift the room.

His Presence Heals

At the end of the day, worship is not about techniques or music—it is about presence. And His presence heals. Exodus 33:14 says, "My presence will go with you, and I will give you rest." That is what wounded souls need—His presence and His rest.

As an inner healing minister, never underestimate the power of worship. Make it central. Let worship prepare the atmosphere, silence the enemy, heal the heart, and open the way for encounters with Jesus.

When people encounter His love in worship, they are changed forever. Chains break. Lies lose power. Sorrow turns to joy. And they walk away not just touched by ministry but transformed by His presence.

Reflection Questions

1. IN WHAT WAYS HAVE I USED WORSHIP AS A "WARM-UP" OR background noise rather than as the central place of encounter? What shift would happen in my ministry if worship became the primary way I usher people into God's presence rather than an optional add-on? Do I treat worship as preparation or as ministry itself? How comfortable am I allowing worship to lead the session instead of my structure? Has God been inviting me to rely more on His presence than on my process?

2. WHEN I PERSONALLY WORSHIP—WHETHER PRIVATELY OR IN ministry—what happens inside me? What distractions, fears, or lies surface, and what does this reveal about how deeply I trust Jesus to meet me (and others) in worship? What parts of worship make me feel vulnerable? Do I worship from rest, or do I strive? How might my private worship life directly impact the atmosphere I carry into ministry rooms?

3. DESCRIBE A TIME WHEN WORSHIP CHANGED THE ATMOSPHERE— either in your heart, your home, or a ministry setting. What specifically shifted, and what does that teach you about the authority worship carries over fear, shame, trauma, and the demonic? What did worship accomplish that your words could not? What does that moment reveal about the role of presence vs. technique? How is God calling you to cultivate this authority in future sessions?

16

DREAMS AND NIGHTMARES

DREAMS ARE ONE OF THE LANGUAGES OF THE SPIRIT. ALL through Scripture, God has spoken to His people through dreams. Jacob dreamed of a ladder reaching to heaven. Joseph dreamed of sheaves and stars bowing. Daniel interpreted the dreams of kings. Joseph, the earthly father of Jesus, was guided four separate times by dreams. Acts 2:17 affirms that in the last days, God will pour out His Spirit and "your old men will dream dreams, your young men will see visions."

But just as God can use dreams for revelation and direction, the enemy also seeks to use them as tools of torment. Trauma often replays itself in nightmares. Fear, shame, or torment may show up night after night. Some people experience demonic oppression in their sleep—night terrors, sleep paralysis, or cycles of nightmares that steal rest and peace.

In inner healing ministry, we must learn to help people invite Jesus into their dream life. Healing is not just for the waking hours. His presence brings restoration even in the night. This chapter will explore how trauma shows up in dreams, how to break cycles of torment, and how to cultivate a lifestyle of encountering Jesus in the night.

How Trauma Shows Up in Dreams

The brain processes pain in the night. That is why people who have suffered trauma often relive it in dreams. Their subconscious replays the scenes, emotions, and fears that were too overwhelming to process at the time. Signs of trauma dreams:

- Recurring nightmares of the same event.
- Dreams where the person feels powerless, trapped, or attacked.
- Dreams replaying abuse, betrayal, or loss.
- Vivid, disturbing images that cause fear or shame upon waking.
- Dreams that leave physical symptoms—sweating, racing heart, exhaustion.

Sometimes the dreams are exact replays. Other times, they are symbolic. A person abused as a child may dream of being chased by monsters. A person who lost a loved one suddenly may dream of endless searching but never finding.

These dreams are not random. They are invitations from the soul for healing. They show where wounds still live. Instead of ignoring them, we bring them to Jesus.

Nightmares and Demonic Torment

Not all nightmares are simply trauma replaying. Some are demonic torment. The enemy loves to invade the night because sleep is meant to be restorative. If he can fill the night with fear, he steals rest and creates cycles of exhaustion. Forms of demonic torment in sleep:

- Night terrors (waking up screaming, paralyzed by fear).
- Sleep paralysis (feeling held down, unable to move or speak).
- Sexual nightmares (succubus/incubus spirits).
- Witchcraft attacks (feeling strangled, visited, or attacked in sleep).
- Repeated tormenting dreams tied to generational curses.

As ministers, we must discern: is this dream trauma processing, or demonic torment? Trauma dreams require healing. Demonic torment requires authority. Often, they overlap—the enemy exploits unhealed wounds to torment in the night.

Breaking Torment Cycles

Cycles of nightmares or torment can feel unbreakable, but Jesus has authority over the night just as much as the day. Psalm 121:4 says, "Behold, He who keeps Israel shall neither slumber nor sleep." God watches over us through the night. Steps to break torment cycles:

1. Identify open doors. Is there unrepented sin, occult involvement, or trauma still unhealed? Close the doors through repentance, forgiveness, and renunciation.
2. Cleanse the atmosphere. Encourage people to anoint their bedroom with oil, dedicate the space to Jesus, and remove occult objects (crystals, dreamcatchers, witchcraft items).

3. Pray protection prayers. Psalm 91, Psalm 4:8 ("In peace I will both lie down and sleep..."), and declarations of angelic covering.
4. Command tormenting spirits to leave. Speak directly: "I break every cycle of nightmares and torment. Every spirit of fear, witchcraft, or perversion must go in Jesus' name."
5. Establish peace. Invite the presence of the Holy Spirit tangibly into the room. Play worship or Scripture audio as they sleep.

Breaking torment cycles often requires persistence. Encourage people to keep standing in prayer until peace reigns.

Inviting Jesus into Dream Life for Healing

One of the most powerful things you can do is help people invite Jesus into their dream life. Many have only experienced the enemy at night. They need to know that God also speaks, heals, and restores in the night. Practical ways:

- Pray before bed. "Jesus, I invite You into my dreams. Heal memories, reveal truth, and speak Your love."
- Presenting Jesus model in dreams. If a nightmare replays trauma, encourage the person to ask: "Jesus, where were You in that memory/dream?" He often reveals Himself even in the dreamscape.
- Ask for prophetic dreams. Encourage them to expect revelation—strategies, encouragement, promises.
- Keep a dream journal. Writing dreams down helps discern patterns and track healing.

Psalm 16:7 says,

"I will bless the Lord who has counseled me; indeed, my mind instructs me in the night."

Night is not wasted—it is a canvas for the Spirit.

Teaching People to Discern Dreams

Not every dream is from God. We generally see three sources of dreams:

1. God-given dreams. Carry revelation, encouragement, or warning.
2. Soul dreams. The brain processing daily life, emotions, or stress.
3. Demonic dreams. Torment, fear, lust, or deception.

Teach people to ask:

- Does this dream line up with Scripture?
- Does it carry peace or fear?
- Does it draw me closer to God or away?

Even nightmares can be redeemed. They show the places that need healing or warfare. Instead of fearing them, we use them as prayer points.

Minister's Role in Dream Healing

As a minister, you can:

- Listen compassionately to dreams without over-interpreting.
- Ask the Holy Spirit for discernment.

- Lead the person to forgive, renounce, or receive truth based on the dream.
- Break demonic ties in prayer.
- Bless them to encounter Jesus in the night.

Never sensationalize dreams. They are not puzzles for entertainment—they are windows into the soul and spirit. Handle them with reverence.

Practical Prayers for Dreams and Nightmares

Here are examples you can use:

Prayer for Healing Dreams:

"Lord, I invite You into my dream life. Heal every place of trauma. Redeem the night as a place of Your presence. Speak truth as I sleep."

Prayer for Protection from Nightmares:

"In Jesus' name, I break every cycle of torment in the night. I command every spirit of fear, witchcraft, or perversion to leave. I cover my mind and body with the blood of Jesus. I declare peace as I sleep."

Prayer for Prophetic Dreams:

"Holy Spirit, I welcome Your voice in the night. Speak to me through dreams. Reveal Your heart, Your strategies, and Your encouragement as I rest."

Testimonies

I've seen people who had nightmares every night for years

experience peace after a single prayer of cleansing and renunciation. One young man tormented by sexual dreams renounced pornography and broke soul ties, received deliverance and immediately the cycle ended.

I've also seen Jesus use dreams for deep healing. A woman who had been abused as a child dreamed of Jesus walking into the memory and holding her younger self. She woke up weeping, but with peace she had never known. The dream became an encounter that sealed her healing.

Redeeming the Night

Psalm 127:2 says, *"He gives His beloved sleep."* That is God's heart. Sleep should not be a place of torment but a place of rest, healing, and revelation.

As inner healing ministers, we must equip people to take back the night. Trauma may surface in dreams, but Jesus heals even there. Demonic torment may invade, but His authority is greater. And when people learn to invite His presence into their dream life, night becomes a place of encounter.

The same Jesus who walks with us in the day watches over us in the night. He is faithful. He heals. He speaks. And He turns nightmares into testimonies of His love.

Reflection Questions

1. WHEN YOU CONSIDER YOUR DREAM LIFE—RECURRING THEMES, emotions, or struggles—what do those dreams reveal about the wounds, fears, or unresolved places in your heart that still need the presence of Jesus? What patterns do I notice in my dreams? Are there repeated emotions (fear, shame, helplessness)? What might my dreams be inviting me to bring into healing?

2. HOW HAVE YOU HISTORICALLY RESPONDED TO NIGHTMARES OR spiritual torment in the night—through fear, avoidance, or resignation—and what would it look like to respond instead with spiritual authority and expectation that Jesus wants to redeem the night? In what ways has fear shaped your view of nighttime? Have you ever treated torment as "normal" instead of something Jesus can heal? What open doors, unhealed wounds, or lies might need closing to reclaim rest?

3. DESCRIBE A MOMENT—WHETHER RECENT OR DISTANT—WHEN God used a dream to reveal, heal, or guide you. What does that experience teach you about God's desire to speak to you in the night, and how might you cultivate a lifestyle of inviting Him into your dreams? What marked you about that dream or encounter? What did you learn about God's voice or His nearness? What practical steps could help you steward dreams more intentionally (journaling, pre-sleep prayer, Scripture meditation)?

17

BODY-SOUL CONNECTION

WHEN GOD CREATED US, HE DIDN'T CREATE THREE SEPARATE compartments called body, soul, and spirit that barely touch each other. He created one integrated being, fearfully and wonderfully made (Psalm 139:14). We are spiritual beings who live in a body and carry a soul. What happens in one part of us affects the others.

That means trauma, wounds, and sin don't just affect emotions or thoughts—they often show up in the physical body. Likewise, physical pain can affect emotions and even spiritual faith. This is why healing ministry must be holistic. If we only address the soul and spirit but ignore the body, people may leave partially healed but still carrying pain that keeps them feeling stuck.

In this chapter, we'll look at how trauma manifests in the body, how to minister body alignment alongside soul healing, and how to pray for holistic wholeness.

How Trauma Manifests in the Body

Trauma isn't only a memory stored in the mind. It's stored in the body. Modern science has discovered what Scripture has hinted at all along: our bodies carry the weight of our experiences. Proverbs 14:30 NIV says, *"A heart at peace gives life to the body, but envy rots the bones."* The state of the soul impacts the body. Common ways trauma shows up physically:

- Chronic pain. Back pain, neck pain, or migraines often tied to unprocessed stress or unforgiveness.
- Autoimmune issues. The body attacking itself, often paralleling inner self-hatred or unresolved grief.
- Digestive problems. Anxiety and trauma disrupting the gut, leading to IBS, ulcers, or nausea.
- Muscle tension. Shoulders locked tight, jaw clenched, body on high alert long after the danger has passed.
- Sleep disorders. Nightmares, insomnia, or restless sleep tied to unhealed wounds.

These physical symptoms are not "all in their head." They are real, tangible, and painful. But they are also signals that something deeper is at work.

Biblical Understanding of Body-Soul Connection

Scripture doesn't separate body and soul. The psalmists often prayed for healing of both together. Psalm 31:9 NIV says, *"Be merciful to me, Lord, for I am in distress; my eyes grow weak with sorrow, my soul and body with grief."* Notice how grief affected both soul and body.

Jesus also modeled holistic healing. He didn't just cast out demons or preach truth—He healed physical sickness. He cared for the whole person. When the paralytic was lowered through the roof (Mark 2:1–12), Jesus forgave his sins (soul and spirit) and healed his body. Both were restored.

In healing ministry, we follow the same model. We invite Jesus to restore spirit, soul, and body together.

Ministering Body Alignment Alongside Soul Healing

When ministering inner healing, it's often wise to also address the body.

Step 1: Identify the Root

Ask the person:

- "When did this pain or condition begin?"
- "Was there a traumatic event around that time?"
- "Do you feel this pain increase when certain emotions surface?"

Often the body pain is directly connected to a soul wound. Example: A woman with chronic neck pain may realize it began after years of carrying shame from abuse.

Step 2: Present the Wound to Jesus

Lead them through forgiveness, repentance, or renunciation as needed. Invite Jesus into the memory. Let Him heal the soul wound.

Step 3: Pray for the Body

Once the soul door is closed, pray over the body with authority:

- "In Jesus' name, I command this trauma stored in the body to be released."
- "I speak to every muscle carrying tension: peace, be still."
- "I declare alignment over the immune system, nervous system, and hormones."

Step 4: Check for Change

Ask the person: "How does your body feel now?" Celebrate even small shifts. Sometimes healing is instant. Sometimes it unfolds over days.

Practical Ministry Examples

- Back pain from unforgiveness. A man carried years of bitterness toward his father. When he forgave, his back pain lifted instantly. His body had been carrying what his heart wouldn't release.
- Autoimmune disorder tied to self-hatred. A woman who had struggled with shame for years renounced the lie "I hate myself" and declared truth. As she did, her symptoms began to lessen.
- Jaw tension tied to unspoken grief. A person clenched their teeth every night. When they finally wept before the Lord and lamented a loss, the tension released.

These aren't formulas—they are testimonies of what happens when body and soul are ministered together.

Prayers for Holistic Wholeness

Here are some examples you can use when ministering:

Prayer for Releasing Trauma in the Body:

"Lord Jesus, I invite You to touch every place in this body that is carrying trauma. I command stored fear, tension, and stress to be released now. I declare peace over the nervous system, peace over the muscles, peace over the mind. Holy Spirit, fill every place with Your presence."

Prayer for Chronic Pain:

"In Jesus' name, I speak to this pain. I command it to lift and leave now. I break every tie between this pain and the wounds of the past. I declare freedom over the body. By His stripes we are healed."

Prayer for Autoimmune Conditions:

"Father, I break the agreement of self-hatred. I declare this body is not the enemy. It is the temple of the Holy Spirit. I command the immune system to come into alignment with heaven. I release life and healing into every cell."

Prayer for Rest and Sleep:

"Lord, I bless this mind and body with peace. I rebuke nightmares, anxiety, and insomnia. I declare Psalm 4:8*: 'In peace I will lie down and sleep, for You alone, Lord, make me dwell in safety.'"

Minister's Posture

When praying for the body-soul connection:

---

* NIV

- Stay compassionate. Don't suggest their pain is "just emotional." Validate it.
- Stay Spirit-led. Ask the Holy Spirit what the root is —sometimes it's trauma, sometimes purely physical.
- Stay holistic. Encourage medical care when needed. Ministry and medicine are not enemies.
- Stay humble. Remember it's Jesus who heals, not your method.

Equipping People to Walk in Wholeness

After ministry, encourage people to:

- Continue forgiving quickly and living in peace.
- Practice worship and rest to keep stress low.
- Declare Scriptures of healing daily.
- Care for their body with sleep, nutrition, and exercise—these are spiritual too.

When people learn to care for spirit, soul, and body together, healing becomes sustainable.

Shalom—Nothing Missing, Nothing Broken

The Hebrew word for peace, shalom, doesn't just mean calm feelings. It means wholeness—nothing missing, nothing broken. That is God's design for us: to be whole in body, soul, and spirit.

Trauma may have fractured the connection. Pain may have taken root in the body. But Jesus came to restore shalom. He heals emotions, renews minds, and restores bodies.

As inner healing ministers, we carry His heart for wholeness. When we minister to both soul and body, we release the fullness of His healing. And people walk away not just relieved in spirit, but refreshed in body, renewed in mind, and whole in every part.

Reflection Questions

1. WHEN YOU LOOK AT THE PLACES WHERE YOUR BODY CARRIES tension, pain, or exhaustion, what emotions or unresolved experiences might be connected to those physical symptoms—and what might Jesus be inviting you to bring into His healing today? What pain or tension seems to "flare up" during stress? What experiences or memories come to mind when you focus on that area? What could healing look like if Jesus touched both the pain and the root?

2. HOW HAVE YOU HISTORICALLY VIEWED YOUR BODY—SOMETHING to ignore, control, shame, push through, or bless—and how does the revelation that your body carries emotional and spiritual meaning reshape how you see yourself and how God sees you? Was I taught to disconnect from my body? Do I view my body as a burden instead of the temple of the Holy Spirit? What would it look like to invite Jesus to heal not just the soul wound but my relationship *with* my body?

3. CAN YOU RECALL A MOMENT WHEN YOUR BODY RESPONDED (positively or negatively) during prayer, worship, or healing—such as peace, trembling, crying, tension releasing, warmth—and what does that experience reveal about the way God ministers to the whole person? How did God meet you through the body, not just the mind? How might physical responses be invitations into deeper healing? What does it show about the integrated way God created us?

18

DISCERNING WHEN IT'S INNER HEALING VS. DELIVERANCE

ONE OF THE MOST IMPORTANT SKILLS FOR AN INNER HEALING minister is discernment. Not every struggle is demonic. Not every struggle is just emotional pain. Often, the two are interwoven. Trauma creates wounds in the soul, and those wounds can become open doors for demonic oppression. At the same time, demonic presence can intensify trauma, fear, and shame.

If we only ever treat everything as a demon, we will miss the heart that needs comfort and healing. If we only ever treat everything as inner pain, we will leave people bound by unchallenged spirits. The true work of ministry is learning to discern the difference and knowing how to flow between inner healing and deliverance as the Holy Spirit leads.

This chapter will unpack the signs of soul pain vs. demonic presence, how to flow between the two, and how to know when to pause, shift, or call in additional help.

Signs of Soul Pain

Soul pain shows up as emotions, lies, and wounds that have not been healed. These may manifest in dramatic ways, but the root is still a broken heart rather than a possessing spirit. Indicators of soul pain:

- Crying or weeping. Tears often signal grief or sadness that needs comfort, not deliverance.
- Sadness or heaviness. The person may feel sorrowful or numb, pointing to wounds needing Jesus' love.
- Shame or self-hatred. Lies about identity surface, requiring truth and renewal.
- Memories surfacing. Trauma being relived or reprocessed, requiring Jesus to enter the memory.
- Protectors or dissociation. Parts of the person carrying pain, needing to be led to Jesus.

In these moments, commanding demons will usually produce little fruit. What's needed is the presenting Jesus model—helping the person invite Him into the pain, hear His truth, forgive, and release.

Signs of Demonic Presence

On the other hand, there are times when what surfaces is not simply soul pain but an unclean spirit resisting freedom. Indicators of demonic presence:

- Hostile manifestations. Growling, snarling, mocking, or speaking in another voice.
- Resistance to prayer. The person cannot say the name of Jesus or refuses to engage.
- Physical contortions. Sudden twisting, violent movements, or paralysis.

- Tormenting voices. Words like "They're mine!" or "I won't leave!" that come with a sense of otherness.
- Unexplainable supernatural phenomena. Unusual strength, dark presence, or manifestations inconsistent with ordinary emotion.

These signs call for authority. Jesus gave us power to cast out demons (Mark 16:17). When a spirit manifests, we don't coddle it—we confront it in His name.

How to Flow Between the Two

Most ministry situations are not purely one or the other. Trauma and spirits intertwine. A person may start by crying (soul pain), then suddenly shift to mocking or violent behavior (demonic presence). Or a demon may surface, and once cast out, deep grief or shame comes forward.

The key is flexibility. Inner healing and deliverance are not competing ministries—they are complementary. Jesus heals the brokenhearted and sets captives free (Luke 4:18). Sometimes He does one first, then the other, and sometimes He weaves them together in the same session.

Practical flow:

1. Start with the heart. Begin with presenting Jesus into the pain.
2. Watch for shifts. If the atmosphere changes from sadness to hostility or mockery, switch to deliverance authority.
3. After deliverance, return to healing. Ask the person: "What are you feeling now? Any memories or

emotions surfacing?" Often the demon was guarding a wound. That wound still needs Jesus.
4. Move back and forth as needed. Don't be rigid. Follow the Spirit.

When to Pause

Sometimes you will need to pause ministry. This is not failure—it is wisdom. Pause when:

- The person is overwhelmed and cannot continue safely.
- The environment is not safe (public place, lack of privacy).
- The ministering team is exhausted or not in unity.
- The person needs medical or professional support alongside ministry.

Pausing allows you to protect the person and the integrity of the ministry. Always frame it positively: "We're going to pause and let Jesus continue the work over time."

When to Shift

There are moments when you realize you're in the wrong mode. If you've been pressing for inner healing but the manifestations are clearly demonic, shift into deliverance. If you've been commanding spirits but all that's surfacing is trauma and grief, shift into inner healing.

Shifting shows humility and discernment. Don't be afraid to say: "Let's change direction. I think Jesus wants to meet you in this pain rather than casting something out right now."

When to Call in Help

No minister should carry this work alone. Some situations are too complex, intense, or overwhelming to handle solo. Call in help when:

- The manifestations are violent or unsafe.
- Multiple layers of dissociation are present and you are inexperienced.
- Ritual abuse survivors need specialized care.
- The person needs deliverance beyond your current authority or training.

Having a covering, a team, and seasoned leaders to lean on is essential. Jesus sent His disciples two by two for a reason.

Guardrails for Discernment

To keep yourself grounded:

- Stay Spirit-led. Ask constantly: "Holy Spirit, is this a wound or a spirit?"
- Don't assume. Just because someone manifests doesn't mean it's demonic—it could be deep trauma.
- Look for fruit. If healing brings peace, stay with it. If authority brings freedom, continue.
- Remain humble. You don't need to prove your power. Your job is to follow Jesus' lead.

Practical Examples

- Case 1: Soul pain only. A woman wept, saying, "I feel worthless." No demons manifested. She forgave her father, invited Jesus into the memory, and received peace. Deliverance wasn't needed.

- Case 2: Demonic presence. A man began growling when we prayed. His body contorted, and a voice shouted, "He's mine!" That was not soul pain—it was a demon. We commanded it to leave, and it did. Afterward, he shared memories of trauma. Then we led him into inner healing.
- Case 3: Both interwoven. A young woman began crying about abuse. Suddenly, her voice shifted, mocking us. We cast the demon out. Immediately, grief surfaced, and she sobbed as Jesus comforted her. Both ministries were needed.

Jesus Heals the Whole Person

At the end of the day, the goal is not to categorize every situation perfectly. The goal is freedom. Jesus came to heal the brokenhearted and set captives free. Inner healing and deliverance are two sides of the same coin.

As ministers, our job is to stay sensitive, humble, and Spirit-led. Sometimes we'll bring Jesus into the memory. Sometimes we'll bind and cast out a demon. Sometimes we'll do both in the same hour.

The key is discernment. The Holy Spirit is faithful to guide us. When we follow His lead, people experience holistic freedom—soul wounds healed, lies broken, demons gone, and identity restored in Christ.

That is the fullness of the gospel of the Kingdom. That is what it means to walk in the ministry of Jesus.

Reflection Questions

1. LOOKING BACK ON MOMENTS WHERE YOU STRUGGLED—emotionally, mentally, or spiritually—can you identify times when what you were experiencing felt more like inner pain than spiritual attack, or more like spiritual attack than inner pain? What does that reveal about how God may want to refine your discernment? What patterns do I see in my own battles? When did comfort and presence bring relief? When did authority and warfare bring relief? What does this show me about how my soul and spirit interact?

2. HOW DO YOU TEND TO REACT WHEN SOMEONE YOU ARE ministering to suddenly shifts—from tears to hostility, from grief to defiance, or from peace to agitation? What does this reveal about your comfort level, your assumptions, and your dependence on the Holy Spirit in real-time ministry moments? Do I default to inner healing or deliverance? Do I freeze when things shift? Do I rely on formulas or on the Spirit? What might Jesus be inviting me to grow in?

3. WHO ARE THE PEOPLE IN YOUR LIFE OR MINISTRY CONTEXT THAT you can call on when sessions become too heavy, complex, or layered—and what does your willingness or unwillingness to involve others reveal about your humility, safety, and alignment with Jesus' model of ministry? Do I minister alone too often? Do I struggle to admit when I need help? Who is part of my covering or team? How does community increase discernment and safety?

PART IV

AFTERCARE
AND GROWTH

19

REBUILDING IDENTITY
AND PURPOSE

EVERY WOUND THE ENEMY INFLICTS CARRIES THE SAME intention: to distort identity and derail purpose. Abuse whispers, "You're worthless." Abandonment whispers, "You're unwanted." Betrayal whispers, "You'll never trust again." Trauma shapes lies that become identities: victim, failure, rejected, abandoned, dirty. These false names become lenses through which people see themselves and their future.

But Jesus didn't just come to forgive sin or heal wounds. He came to restore identity and purpose. He came to give us a new name, a new nature, and a new mission. Isaiah 62:2 says, "You shall be called by a new name, which the mouth of the Lord will name." Revelation 2:17 says that to the one who overcomes, He will give a white stone with a new name written on it. Identity is not an afterthought in healing—it is the destination.

This chapter will walk through how to rebuild identity and purpose after healing. We will look at receiving a new name and identity in Christ, using prophetic acts and declarations to seal restoration, and learning to live from sonship instead of wounds.

Receiving a New Name and Identity in Christ

One of the most consistent patterns in Scripture is God renaming people.

- Abram became Abraham. (Gen. 17:5)
- Sarai became Sarah. (Gen. 17:15)
- Jacob became Israel. (Gen. 32:28)
- Simon became Peter. (John 1:42)
- Saul became Paul. (Acts 13:9)

Why does God do this? Because names carry identity. The old name represented old patterns, wounds, or limitations. The new name represents God's destiny and design.

In inner healing, part of the restoration process is helping people hear what God calls them. After wounds are healed and lies are broken, ask:

- "Jesus, what do You call them?"
- "What name do You give them in this season?"
- "What truth do You want them to carry forward?"

This could be a single word: "Beloved." It could be a phrase: "Faithful one." It could be a Scripture: "More than a conqueror." What matters is that it comes from His mouth.

Encourage people to write down their new name or identity declaration. Have them declare it daily. Help them replace the old label with the new truth. If they hear "rejected," teach them to declare: "I am chosen in Christ before the foundation of the world." If they hear "dirty," declare: "I am washed, sanctified, and justified by the blood of Jesus."

Prophetic Acts and Declarations of Restoration

Sometimes words alone are not enough. The Bible is full of prophetic acts—physical actions that demonstrate spiritual truth. Jeremiah smashed a clay pot to symbolize judgment (Jer. 19:10). Elisha threw salt into water to heal it (2 Kings 2:21). Jesus broke bread to reveal His body. Prophetic acts can help seal identity restoration:

- Writing and tearing. Write old lies on paper ("worthless," "unlovable"), then tear them up and throw them away.
- Stone exchange. Give the person a white stone (Revelation 2:17) and have them write their new name on it.
- Garment exchange. Have them remove a shawl or cloth symbolizing shame and put on a new one symbolizing righteousness (Isaiah 61:10).
- Mirror declarations. Have them look in a mirror and declare their new identity daily.

Declarations are equally powerful. Proverbs 18:21 says, "Death and life are in the power of the tongue." When people declare truth out loud, they retrain their soul and resist the enemy's lies. Examples:

- "I am a beloved child of God."
- "I am forgiven and free."
- "I am chosen, called, and sent."
- "I am seated with Christ in heavenly places."

- "I am more than a conqueror through Him who loves me."

Encourage people to build a daily rhythm of declaring identity until it becomes natural.

Living from Sonship Instead of Wounds

The ultimate goal of inner healing is not just relief from pain but restoration to sonship. Romans 8:15 NIV says, "*The Spirit you received brought about your adoption to sonship. And by Him we cry, 'Abba, Father.'*" Living from wounds looks like:

- Constantly reacting from fear, shame, or rejection.
- Building identity around what happened rather than what God says.
- Striving to earn love, approval, or security.
- Remaining stuck in cycles of self-sabotage.

Living from sonship looks like:

- Resting in the Father's love.
- Knowing you are secure in Christ regardless of circumstances.
- Responding from peace instead of reacting from pain.
- Walking confidently in your God-given authority and purpose.

As ministers, we must not just help people heal wounds—we must disciple them into sonship. Help them see themselves as sons and daughters, not survivors or victims. Encourage them to cultivate intimacy with the Father, walk in the Spirit, and align with their Kingdom purpose.

Practical Ministry Flow

Here's how you can walk someone through rebuilding identity and purpose:

1. Close wounds. Lead them through healing and forgiveness for the pain.
2. Ask Jesus for identity. "Jesus, what do You call them?"
3. Receive new name. Have them write it down or speak it out.
4. Prophetic act. Do a symbolic act to seal the truth (stone, garment, tearing lies).
5. Declaration. Have them declare truth out loud.
6. Activation. Encourage them to live as a son/daughter —making decisions, building relationships, and pursuing purpose from this new identity.

Minister's Posture

When walking people into new identity:

- Celebrate. Rejoice with them as they receive truth. Heaven rejoices over every restoration.
- Affirm. Remind them consistently of their identity when doubts arise.
- Guard humility. Identity in Christ produces confidence without pride.
- Stay anchored in Scripture. Root new names in biblical truth.

From Wounds to Destiny

Revelation 21:5 says, "Behold, I make all things new." That is the banner over identity restoration. The enemy sought to define people by their pain. Jesus redefines them by His purpose.

Healing is not complete until identity is rebuilt and destiny is restored. People are not just freed from something—they are freed for something. Freed from shame, for sonship. Freed from lies, for truth. Freed from despair, for purpose.

As ministers, our role is to walk with them through the exchange. From wounds to new names. From false identities to true sonship. From brokenness to Kingdom purpose.

This is the joy of inner healing: seeing people rise not just healed, but whole, confident, and ready to live as beloved sons and daughters of the King.

Reflection Questions

1. WHAT NAMES—SPOKEN BY OTHERS, SHAPED BY TRAUMA, OR whispered by the enemy—have tried to define you throughout your life, and how have those false identities affected the way you see yourself, relate to others, and approach your purpose? What labels still echo in my thoughts? What patterns or behaviors are connected to those old names? How have those names limited my confidence, intimacy with God, or calling?

2. WHEN YOU ASK JESUS, "WHAT DO YOU CALL ME?" WHAT DO you sense Him revealing—through Scripture, His presence, or the witness of the Spirit—and what would it look like to actually *live* from that new name in your daily choices, relationships, and purpose? What new name or identity word is He highlighting? How does this new name confront or replace the old ones? What would change if I fully embraced this identity —not just spiritually, but practically?

3. IN WHAT AREAS OF YOUR LIFE DO YOU STILL FIND YOURSELF reacting from wounds—fear, rejection, shame, defensiveness, striving—rather than responding from sonship, and what steps can you take to intentionally live from the love, security, and authority of being a son or daughter of the Father? Where does fear still steer my decisions? Where do I still feel like I must prove myself or earn affection? What habits or declarations would help me shift from wounded living to Kingdom living?

20

THE ROLE OF COMMUNITY

INNER HEALING IS POWERFUL, BUT IT WAS NEVER MEANT TO happen in isolation. Healing moments in the presence of God are beautiful, but if a person leaves those moments and goes back to loneliness, toxic environments, or isolation, much of what God did can be undermined. We were not created to walk alone. We were created for family. We were created for community.

That's why one of the most important roles of an inner healing minister is not just to help people encounter Jesus in their wounds but to connect them into a community where they can walk out their freedom. The Kingdom is not just about deliverance from the past—it's about discipleship into a new way of living.

In this chapter, we'll look at why belonging matters after healing, how the house church model provides safe spaces for discipleship, and how community becomes the environment for integration and growth.

Why Belonging Matters After Healing

Belonging is not optional. It is essential. God Himself said in Genesis 2:18 NIV, "*It is not good for man to be alone.*" That was not just about marriage—it was about human design. We are wired for connection.

After inner healing, people are often tender and vulnerable. Old lies have been broken. Wounds have been touched. But that very vulnerability can make them a target for the enemy if they are not rooted in healthy community. Belonging provides:

- Safety. A place where they are accepted and loved as they walk out freedom.
- Accountability. Others who can encourage them to keep choosing truth.
- Discipleship. Ongoing teaching, correction, and growth.
- Healing in relationship. Much of our pain comes through relationships, and much of our healing is completed through healthy ones.

Community is the soil where healing takes root. Without it, people risk falling back into old patterns. With it, they grow into maturity.

House Church Model: Safe Spaces for Discipleship

In SOZO Church, we use the house church model, and I believe it's one of the best ways to create safe spaces for discipleship after healing. Some call them small groups, but for us, house churches are more than just Bible studies. They are micro-expressions of the church, led by spiritually mature and submitted disciples who are fully trained to minister the life of Jesus. A healthy house church provides:

- Spiritual family. People know your name, your story, and your journey.
- All of Jesus' ministry. Leaders are equipped to preach, teach, heal the sick, cast out demons, counsel marriages, and disciple believers.
- Safe space. A living room feels less intimidating than a stage. People can process their story without shame.
- Accessibility. We encourage people to join the house church closest to where they live, so they're not driving past three communities to get to one. Local connection matters.

When someone goes through healing or deliverance, my consistent encouragement is this: get planted in a house church. That's where you will grow roots. That's where you will be discipled. That's where you will have people walk with you when the next layer of healing surfaces.

Community for Integration and Growth

Healing moments are catalytic, but integration happens in community. Integration means learning to live from the new identity instead of the old wounds. It means practicing forgiveness daily, walking in truth consistently, and choosing healthy patterns of relationship. Community provides the environment where integration happens:

- Practicing new identity. In community, people test out their new identity. If Jesus renamed them

"Beloved," they get to walk as beloved in real relationships.

- Opportunities to forgive. Community always involves conflict. That conflict becomes practice ground for forgiveness.
- Accountability in truth. When lies resurface, brothers and sisters can remind them of what Jesus said.
- Celebration of growth. Testimonies shared in community build faith and joy.
- Ongoing discipleship. Leaders help them continue in Scripture, prayer, and obedience.

Healing is not an event—it's a lifestyle. And community is what sustains the lifestyle.

Practical Steps for Ministers

As an inner healing minister, don't stop at the session. Help people connect into community.

- Ask directly. "Do you have a house church or small group you're part of?"
- Encourage locally. Connect them with the nearest group, not just your own.
- Follow up. Check in a few weeks later and ask if they've joined.
- Support leaders. Make sure house church leaders are equipped to handle continued ministry needs.
- Celebrate testimonies. Share with the larger church how people are growing through community.

Your role is not just to heal but to plant people in family.

That's what Jesus did. He didn't just minister to individuals—He formed a community of disciples.

Minister's Posture

As you point people toward community:

- Stay Kingdom-minded. Don't hoard people for your own group—send them where they will grow.
- Stay patient. Some resist community because of past wounds. Encourage gently but persistently.
- Stay relational. Healing flows best in family, not in programs.
- Stay faithful. Model what you ask others to do by staying planted in community yourself.

Healing Belongs in Family

At the end of the day, inner healing is not complete until it is rooted in community. Jesus heals individuals, but He always plants them in family. The early church lived this out in Acts 2:42–47, gathering in homes, breaking bread, praying, and sharing life. And the fruit was explosive growth and sustained transformation.

If we want to see lasting healing, we must build communities where people can belong, be discipled, and grow. House churches, small groups, spiritual families—these are not optional extras. They are essential to the Kingdom.

Healing happens in encounters. Wholeness happens in community. As ministers, our job is not done until the broken are planted in family, discipled into maturity, and walking out their freedom in the context of the body of Christ.

Reflection Questions

1. WHAT HAS COMMUNITY MEANT TO YOU THROUGHOUT YOUR LIFE —both positively and negatively—and how have your past experiences with relationships, family, or churches shaped the way you engage (or avoid) community today? Do I tend to isolate when I'm hurting? What fears or expectations influence how I show up in groups? How have past wounds shaped my view of spiritual family?

2. WHEN YOU THINK ABOUT THE HEALING JESUS HAS DONE IN your life, what new patterns, habits, or ways of relating to others do you need a community to help you practice, reinforce, or walk out—and what becomes difficult or vulnerable if you try to do it alone? What parts of my identity need encouragement from others? What lies tend to resurface when I'm isolated? How does community help me walk in truth, forgiveness, or accountability?

3. WHO ARE THE PEOPLE, GROUPS, OR SPIRITUAL FAMILIES YOU sense the Holy Spirit inviting you to connect with more deeply —and what steps can you take to move toward them, even if doing so challenges old fears, patterns, or comfort zones? Where is God planting me right now? What relational risks might I need to take? What would obedience look like in terms of connection, vulnerability, or belonging?

21

BOUNDARIES AND REPARENTING THE SOUL

ONE OF THE MOST CRUCIAL PARTS OF SUSTAINED INNER HEALING IS learning how to live differently after the wound has been addressed. If someone is healed but never learns new ways of relating, they are vulnerable to slipping back into cycles of abuse, unhealthy relationships, or self-sabotage. Healing is not just freedom from the past; it is training for the future.

Two areas are especially vital for this ongoing journey: boundaries and reparenting the soul. Boundaries help people protect what God has restored. Reparenting helps them experience the nurturing, safety, and guidance that may have been missing in childhood, but which God Himself provides as a loving Father. Without these, healed hearts can easily become wounded again. With them, healed hearts grow into mature, rooted, and fruitful lives.

Teaching Healthy Boundaries After Abuse

Many people who have experienced abuse—whether sexual, emotional, physical, or spiritual—struggle with boundaries. Abuse violates boundaries. It trains people to believe they have no right to say no, no right to be safe, no right to protect themselves. As a result, survivors often fall into one of two traps:

1. No boundaries at all. They allow people to walk over them, use them, or control them.
2. Walls instead of boundaries. They shut everyone out completely, trusting no one.

Both extremes keep them from living in wholeness. Boundaries are not about selfishness—they are about stewardship. Proverbs 4:23 NIV says, *"Above all else, guard your heart, for everything you do flows from it."*

Keys to teaching boundaries:

- Boundaries honor God. They say, "My life is valuable because I belong to Him."
- Boundaries protect healing. They prevent re-exposure to toxic cycles.
- Boundaries define responsibility. They clarify what is mine to carry and what is not.
- Boundaries create freedom. They allow love to flourish without fear of control.

Practical examples:

- Saying "no" without guilt.
- Refusing to stay in abusive relationships.
- Learning to walk away from manipulation or control.
- Choosing safe people who respect their yes and their no.

As ministers, we must equip people with both the biblical foundation and practical language for boundaries. For some, the most spiritual step they can take is to say "no" for the first time without shame.

Helping Inner Children Experience God's Reparenting

Another vital aspect of sustained healing is what I call reparenting the soul. Many people's wounds come from unmet childhood needs—safety, nurture, affection, affirmation, discipline. When those needs are not met, the inner child remains wounded, still longing for what was missing.

God Himself promises to reparent us. Psalm 27:10 NIV says, *"Though my father and mother forsake me, the Lord will receive me."* He is the perfect Father, and through His Spirit, He meets the needs left unmet by earthly parents.

How to guide people into reparenting encounters:

- Acknowledge the lack. Invite them to name what was missing (love, safety, provision).
- Invite Jesus to fill it. Ask: "Jesus, will You show Yourself as the perfect Father here?"
- Nurturing experiences. Encourage them to see Jesus holding their inner child, speaking words of affirmation, giving gifts of love.
- Integration. Lead them to embrace that child within, no longer ignored or rejected, but loved and healed in Christ.

This is not childish—it is discipleship. It is allowing the Spirit of adoption to cry out, *"Abba, Father"* (Rom. 8:15), and to heal the orphan places inside.

Avoiding Retrauma and Codependency

As powerful as inner healing is, there are dangers if people are not taught to walk wisely afterward. Two dangers stand out: retrauma and codependency.

Retrauma

Retrauma happens when people step back into the same toxic environments that wounded them in the first place. If someone goes back to abusive relationships, unhealthy churches, or destructive patterns, the wound can reopen. That is why boundaries matter so much. Healing must be protected. As ministers, we must encourage people:

- Don't rush back into unsafe relationships.
  Forgiveness doesn't mean immediate reconciliation.
- Choose safe community. Root yourself in people
  who honor your healing.
- Pace your growth. Don't overwhelm yourself with
  too much too fast.

Codependency

Codependency happens when people lean on others to fill needs only God can meet. It shows up as dependency on a leader, friend, or minister to feel valuable, safe, or loved. While community is vital, codependency is dangerous because it replaces God with people. Signs of codependency:

- Needing constant reassurance.
- Feeling responsible for others' emotions.
- Losing identity in serving or pleasing others.
- Depending on a minister instead of Jesus.

As ministers, we must point people back to Christ. Encourage them to cultivate their own relationship with Jesus, their own hearing of His voice, their own confidence in His love. Remind them: community supports healing, but only God sustains it.

Practical Ministry Tools

Here are ways you can practically lead people into boundaries and reparenting:

- Boundary declarations. Have them say: "I am valuable. I am allowed to say no. I choose safe relationships."
- Roleplay boundaries. Practice saying no in a safe space so they gain confidence.
- Reparenting prayers. Lead them: "Father, I invite You to show me what I needed as a child. Will You give it to me now?"
- Inner child affirmation. Encourage them to picture hugging their younger self with Jesus present, speaking words like, "It's not your fault. You are loved. You are safe now."
- Community accountability. Connect them to safe groups where boundaries are respected and love is genuine.

Minister's Posture

When ministering in these areas:

- Be gentle. Boundaries and reparenting touch deep, tender places.

- Be patient. People may resist boundaries because of fear of rejection.
- Be wise. Guard against dependency on you—always point to Jesus.
- Be encouraging. Celebrate small steps. Every "no" and every encounter with the Father is progress.

Growing Into Mature Sons and Daughters

Inner healing doesn't end with wounds being touched. It continues as people learn to live differently. Boundaries protect healing. Reparenting fills what was missing. Together, they establish people as mature sons and daughters of God who are no longer defined by abuse, orphanhood, or brokenness.

The Father is raising up a generation who know how to say no with grace, yes with love, and live as beloved children secure in His arms. As ministers, our role is to help them not only receive healing but grow into maturity—no longer victims, no longer orphans, but sons and daughters walking in wholeness, purpose, and freedom.

Reflection Questions

1. IN WHAT WAYS HAVE YOUR PAST WOUNDS SHAPED HOW YOU relate to people today—either by having no boundaries or by building walls—and how is the Holy Spirit inviting you to create healthier, God-honoring boundaries now? Where do I tend to overextend myself or allow others to cross lines? Where do I shut down, withdraw, or avoid vulnerability? What would it look like for me to protect what God has healed without isolating myself?

2. WHAT UNMET NEEDS FROM YOUR CHILDHOOD STILL INFLUENCE your emotions, reactions, or relationships—and what might it look like for you to invite Jesus to reparent and nurture those places of your heart? What did I need but never receive (safety, affirmation, comfort, guidance)? How does my "inner child" still react in ways that belong to old wounds? What is Jesus wanting to give me now that my earthly parents could not?

3. IN YOUR CURRENT SEASON, WHERE ARE YOU MOST VULNERABLE to retrauma or codependency—and what steps can you take to walk in maturity, ownership, and sonship rather than slipping back into old patterns or unhealthy dependencies? What environments or relationships do I need to avoid or redefine? Where am I tempted to rely too heavily on another person instead of God? How can I cultivate a rhythm of personal intimacy, boundaries, and wise connection?

22

SPIRITUAL DISCIPLINES
FOR WHOLENESS

INNER HEALING IS NEVER MEANT TO BE A ONE-TIME EVENT. IT'S AN ongoing lifestyle of walking with Jesus, renewing the mind, and practicing rhythms that keep the soul anchored in His presence. Freedom must be guarded. Healing must be stewarded. And the way we do that is through spiritual disciplines.

Spiritual disciplines are not about striving or earning God's love. They are about creating consistent rhythms that open our hearts to His grace. They are about aligning our lives with the reality that healing comes from abiding in Him. Jesus said in John 15:5, *"Apart from Me you can do nothing."* Disciplines keep us connected to the Vine so that fruit can remain.

In this chapter, we'll look at daily practices of the Word, prayer, and journaling, rhythms of rest, worship, and accountability, and ongoing habits that sustain inner healing and wholeness.

Daily Word

The Word of God is the foundation of wholeness. Lies are broken, wounds are healed, and truth takes root when people anchor themselves in Scripture. Psalm 1 says that the one who meditates on the Word day and night is like a tree planted by streams of water, bearing fruit in every season. Practical steps:

- Daily reading. Even a few verses meditated on deeply can shift the heart.
- Identity Scriptures. Focus on passages that affirm identity in Christ (Eph. 1, Rom. 8).
- Speaking the Word. Read aloud to let truth reshape the atmosphere.
- Writing verses. Journal key Scriptures and declare them over your life.

When people renew their minds with the Word daily, lies lose power and wholeness becomes their default.

Daily Prayer

Prayer is not just talking—it is communion with the Father. After healing, people need ongoing conversation with God to stay rooted in His love and truth. Practical rhythms:

- Morning prayer. Begin the day with surrender and listening: "Lord, here I am. Speak to me."
- Breath prayers. Simple prayers throughout the day: "Jesus, I trust You." "Holy Spirit, fill me."
- Evening reflection. End the day by asking, "Lord, where did I see You today? Where do I need Your peace?"

Encourage people not to complicate prayer. Teach them to

talk honestly, listen quietly, and invite the Spirit into every moment.

Journaling

Journaling is one of the most practical tools to sustain healing. It gives people a place to process emotions, track progress, and record what God is saying. Benefits of journaling:

- Identifying lies. Write down recurring negative thoughts and confront them with Scripture.
- Recording encounters. Capture moments when Jesus speaks or heals.
- Tracking growth. Look back months later to see how far God has brought them.
- Processing emotions. Writing helps bring clarity and release.

Encourage journaling as part of daily devotion. Some of the greatest breakthroughs come not in a session but in the quiet place with pen and paper.

Rhythms of Rest

Many who come for inner healing live in constant stress or striving. They need to learn rhythms of rest. Rest is not laziness —it is trust. God Himself modeled rest by ceasing on the seventh day, not because He was tired but to set a pattern for us. Practical rest rhythms:

- Sabbath. A weekly day set apart for worship, joy, and renewal.
- Sleep. Prioritizing healthy sleep as part of spiritual health.

- Margin. Building breathing room into schedules.
- Play. Allowing space for fun, creativity, and delight.

Rest restores the soul and prevents burnout. It is one of the most spiritual disciplines we can practice.

Worship

Worship must become a lifestyle, not just a Sunday event. Worship shifts atmospheres, silences lies, and opens hearts to God's presence. Encourage people to cultivate personal worship as part of their healing journey. Practical habits:

- Daily worship time. Play songs, sing, or speak words of adoration to Jesus.
- Worship in pain. Choose to exalt God even when emotions are heavy.
- Spontaneous praise. Let worship flow naturally in moments throughout the day.
- Scripture worship. Sing or pray verses like Psalms back to God.

When worship becomes habitual, healing is sustained because the heart stays tender in His presence.

Accountability

Freedom thrives in accountability. James 5:16 ESV says, *"Confess your sins to one another and pray for one another, that you may be healed."* Healing is sustained when people walk with trusted brothers and sisters who encourage, challenge, and cover them. Practical steps:

- Find safe people. Encourage connection with a mentor, leader, or house church.
- Be honest. Share struggles openly to break shame and secrecy.
- Pray together. Regular accountability prayer strengthens weak places.
- Set guardrails. Use accountability for areas of temptation or old patterns.

Accountability is not control—it is partnership. It is brothers and sisters helping each other walk in truth.

Ongoing Practices that Sustain Healing

Wholeness is not maintained by one discipline alone but by a rhythm of practices. Encourage people to build a lifestyle of:

- Daily Word, prayer, journaling. Anchoring in truth.
- Weekly Sabbath and worship. Resting and exalting God.
- Regular accountability. Walking in honesty and community.
- Consistent forgiveness. Quickly releasing offense before it festers.
- Generosity and service. Living outward keeps the heart free from self-focus.

These practices are not burdens—they are life-giving habits that create stability.

Minister's Role

As an inner healing minister, don't just help people through a session—equip them for the journey. Give them practical assignments. Encourage them to start small: one Scripture a day, five minutes of journaling, one worship song. Help them build consistency.

Healing is sustained not by dramatic encounters alone but by steady rhythms of abiding in Christ. Teach people that disciplines are not rules to follow but rhythms that open the door for God's grace daily.

Abiding for Wholeness

At the end of the day, inner healing is about abiding. Jesus said in John 15:7 NIV, *"If you remain in Me and My words remain in you, ask whatever you wish, and it will be done for you."* Wholeness flows from remaining in Him.

Daily Word, prayer, journaling. Rhythms of rest and worship. Community and accountability. These are not optional extras—they are the scaffolding that holds up the healing God has done.

If people will abide in Him, they will not just experience moments of healing but lifestyles of wholeness. And from that place, they will not only stay free but become healers themselves—sons and daughters of God carrying His love, peace, and presence into the world.

Reflection Questions

1. WHICH SPIRITUAL DISCIPLINE—WORD, PRAYER, JOURNALING, rest, worship, or accountability—has been the weakest rhythm in your life, and how has its absence affected your ability to stay rooted in healing and truth? What discipline have I ignored or minimized? How has that created vulnerability to old patterns, lies, or emotional instability? What simple step can I take this week to strengthen that rhythm?

2. WHEN YOU THINK ABOUT ABIDING IN JESUS (JOHN 15), WHAT distractions, habits, or emotional patterns tend to pull you out of His presence—and what practical changes could help you remain connected to Him throughout the day? What drains my spiritual life quickly? What practices actually restore me? What boundaries or changes would help me stay in a place of peace and connection?

3. WHICH VOICES SHAPE YOUR INTERNAL WORLD THE MOST— God's Word, your emotions, past wounds, or the opinions of others—and what would it look like for you to intentionally shift your daily input so that Scripture becomes the loudest voice? What voices do I most easily believe? How can I create a daily environment where God's voice becomes primary? What specific Scriptures do I need to meditate on in this season?

23

PROTECTING THE INNER HEALING MINISTER

INNER HEALING MINISTRY IS ONE OF THE GREATEST PRIVILEGES IN the Kingdom. To watch Jesus heal the brokenhearted, restore shattered identities, and redeem trauma is holy ground. But walking with people through deep pain is not without cost. If we are not careful, the very work of healing can take a toll on the minister.

Many who start strong in this ministry burn out within a few years—not because the call wasn't real, but because they did not learn how to protect their own hearts and lives as they poured into others. Some become cynical, weary, or even traumatized themselves from constantly hearing stories of abuse, betrayal, and trauma. Others drift into isolation, thinking they must carry every burden alone.

That is not the Father's design. Inner healing ministers are called to serve from overflow, not depletion. They are called to walk under covering, not alone. They are called to continue receiving healing themselves, not act as if they have already arrived.

This chapter will equip you with practical and spiritual guardrails to protect yourself as an inner healing minister: guarding against compassion fatigue and secondary trauma, staying under covering and debriefing with a team, and continuing your own journey of healing.

Guarding Against Compassion Fatigue and Secondary Trauma

When you regularly listen to people's pain, you carry the risk of what psychologists call compassion fatigue or secondary trauma.

- Compassion fatigue happens when your heart grows weary from constantly carrying others' burdens. You begin to feel emotionally numb or detached.
- Secondary trauma happens when the stories of others' trauma begin to affect you personally. You may have nightmares, anxiety, or intrusive thoughts about what you've heard.

Both are real dangers in this ministry. If ignored, they can lead to burnout, moral failure, or walking away from the call.

Signs you may be experiencing these:

- Feeling emotionally drained after every session.
- Struggling to care about people the way you once did.
- Having difficulty sleeping because of the stories you've heard.
- Feeling hopeless or cynical about whether people can really change.

- Experiencing increased irritability or withdrawal from relationships.

How to guard against them:

- Set limits. Don't take on more sessions than you can handle. Jesus Himself often withdrew to lonely places to pray (Luke 5:16).
- Practice Sabbath. Rest is not optional—it is a command. Build rhythms of renewal.
- Release burdens quickly. After each session, pray and give the person's pain back to Jesus. Say: "Lord, I release them into Your hands. I will not carry what You alone can carry."
- Stay filled. Worship, prayer, time in the Word— these keep your heart full so you're giving from overflow, not depletion.

Staying Under Covering and Debriefing With Team

Ministry is not meant to be done alone. Jesus sent His disciples out two by two. Paul always traveled with companions. Covering and community are not luxuries—they are safeguards.

Spiritual Covering

Every inner healing minister must be submitted under spiritual authority. This is not control—it is protection. A covering provides:

- Accountability. Someone who can ask you hard questions.

- Spiritual protection. Authority flows through alignment.
- Wisdom. Leaders who have walked the road longer can guide you.

Never minister as a lone ranger. Always stay connected to your local church and spiritual leaders.

Team Debrief

One of the most practical tools for protection is debriefing with your team after ministry sessions. Don't just walk out and go home. Take time to:

- Share what happened.
- Pray for each other.
- Release the burdens together.
- Encourage and affirm one another.

Team debrief helps prevent isolation, provides perspective, and keeps ministry healthy.

Ongoing Healing for Ministers Themselves

Perhaps the most important principle is this: ministers must keep receiving healing themselves. No one "graduates" from needing Jesus' healing. We are all in process. The moment you think you are above needing healing, you are in danger.

Why ministers need ongoing healing:

- Wounds surface at new levels. Marriage, parenting, leadership—all expose new layers that Jesus wants to heal.

- The enemy targets ministers. Attacks are real. Staying healed is protection.
- We minister best from what we've received. Freely you have received, freely give (Matt. 10:8).

How to pursue ongoing healing:

- Regular check-ins. Meet with trusted mentors or peers to share where you are struggling.
- Personal ministry. Be willing to sit in the chair yourself and let others lead you through healing prayer.
- Accountability partners. People who know your weaknesses and walk with you.
- Retreats and rest. Periodic times away with God to refresh and heal.

Your effectiveness as a minister is directly tied to your willingness to keep receiving healing. Stay humble. Stay dependent. Stay open to the Spirit's work in you.

Minister's Posture

To protect yourself as an inner healing minister:

- Stay humble. Remember you are not the Savior—Jesus is.
- Stay honest. Admit when you are weary or triggered.
- Stay connected. Don't isolate. Stay in covering, community, and team.
- Stay filled. Prioritize your own walk with God.
- Stay healed. Pursue ongoing healing for your own wounds.

Longevity in Ministry

The Father is not just interested in using you for a season—He wants you to finish well. He wants you to be like Paul, who said at the end of his life, *"I have fought the good fight, I have finished the race, I have kept the faith"* (2 Tim. 4:7 NIV).

Protecting yourself as an inner healing minister is not selfish—it is stewardship. It ensures that you will still be standing, whole and full of joy, years from now.

Guard against compassion fatigue. Stay under covering and debrief with your team. Keep receiving healing yourself. In doing so, you will not only survive in this ministry—you will thrive. And you will be able to carry Jesus' healing presence to countless others for decades to come.

Reflection Questions

1. In what ways have you noticed signs of compassion fatigue, emotional depletion, or secondary trauma in your ministry—and what rhythms of rest, boundaries, or spiritual practices need to be restored or strengthened to bring your heart back into overflow instead of strain? What symptoms am I ignoring? Where have I slipped into ministering from emptiness instead of abundance? What specific changes (schedule, Sabbath, prayer, sleep, limits) do I need to make?

2. Who are the people—leaders, mentors, peers, or team members—who truly cover you spiritually, know your vulnerabilities, and help carry burdens with you? If any gaps exist, what steps do you need to take to come back under healthy covering and community so you do not walk alone? Am I fully submitted somewhere? Do I intentionally debrief with anyone after heavy sessions? If I am isolated, what practical steps will I take to reconnect?

3. What areas of your own life—old wounds, patterns, triggers, fears, or unhealed places—has the Lord been highlighting that you may have been avoiding, and what would it look like for you to pursue ongoing healing with the same humility and courage you ask others to walk in? What parts of *my* heart need ministry? Why have I delayed dealing with them? Who can I ask to walk me through healing? What would change in my life or ministry if I pursued this healing now?

CONCLUSION
CARRIERS OF HIS HEALING PRESENCE

As we come to the end of this manual, I want to remind you of something vital: this is not just a book about methods or models. It's about a Person. His name is Jesus. He is the Healer, the Deliverer, the Restorer of broken hearts. Everything you have read—every tool, every chapter, every principle—points back to Him.

Inner healing ministry is not about us being wise enough, strong enough, or gifted enough. It is about us being surrendered enough to let Him use us as vessels. It's about creating a safe space where people can encounter the living Christ. He is the One who binds up the brokenhearted, who exchanges ashes for beauty, mourning for joy, and despair for praise (Isaiah 61).

The Call to Heal the Brokenhearted

This ministry is not optional for the church. It is central. Jesus announced His mission in Luke 4:18:

"The Spirit of the Lord is upon Me, because He has anointed Me to preach good news to the poor; He has sent Me to heal the brokenhearted, to proclaim liberty to the captives and recovery of sight to the blind, to set at liberty those who are oppressed."

Healing the brokenhearted is not an add-on. It is the heartbeat of the gospel. When people meet Jesus in their pain, they discover freedom that no program, no medication, no striving could ever produce.

You are stepping into that same mission. You are partnering with heaven to fulfill Isaiah 61 and Luke 4 in your generation.

The Privilege and Weight of the Call

To minister inner healing is to walk on holy ground. You will hear stories of pain that make your heart ache. You will sit with people in the rawest moments of their lives. You will carry burdens with them that are heavy. But you will also witness some of the most beautiful moments imaginable—the moment Jesus steps into a memory, the moment tears of shame turn to tears of joy, the moment a lie that shaped a life for decades is replaced by His truth.

There is no greater privilege than to see the light of Christ break into someone's darkness.

But with privilege comes weight. You must carry this ministry with humility, integrity, and dependence on the Spirit. Never rush. Never pressure. Never make it about you. Your role is to point to Jesus, to hold the lantern while He enters the cave, to be a midwife while He brings new birth.

Commissioned as Ministers of Wholeness

As you finish this manual, I want to commission you in the Spirit:

- You are called to be a safe place for the wounded.
- You are called to be a truth-teller who confronts lies with the Word of God.
- You are called to be a guide who helps people meet Jesus in the broken places.
- You are called to be a warrior who knows how to discern when a demon is present and take authority in Jesus' name.
- You are called to be a father or mother in the faith who nurtures, disciples, and releases others into their purpose.

This is not just about ministry sessions. This is about a lifestyle. Carry His healing presence everywhere you go—into your family, your workplace, your church, your city.

Guarding the Deposit

As you minister, remember to guard what God has entrusted to you. Stay submitted to covering. Stay in community. Stay in the Word and prayer. Keep receiving healing yourself. Protect your heart from pride, burnout, and isolation. Ministry is not a sprint—it is a marathon. Longevity comes from humility and dependence on the Spirit.

Paul told Timothy,

> *"Guard the good deposit that was entrusted to you—guard it with the help of the Holy Spirit who lives in us" (2 Tim. 1:14 NIV).*

Guard this ministry the same way.

A Final Word of Encouragement

Let me leave you with this: you are not alone in this. Jesus said in Matthew 28:20, "I am with you always, even to the end of the age." The same Spirit that raised Christ from the dead lives in you. The angels of God surround you. The covering of the body of Christ supports you.

You may feel inadequate at times. You may feel overwhelmed by the depth of people's pain. But remember this: the pressure is not on you to heal. The pressure is only to obey. Healing is His work. Your job is to make space, to listen, to guide, to declare truth, and to trust Him with the rest.

When you minister from that posture—dependent, surrendered, full of faith—you will see miracles. You will watch chains fall. You will hear the cries of the broken turn into songs of joy. And you will know that you have been faithful to the call.

The Invitation

So here is the invitation: live as a carrier of His healing presence. Make your life an altar where the broken can meet Jesus. Keep your hands open, your heart soft, your ears tuned to His voice. Let compassion flow. Let courage rise. Let humility anchor you.

And as you do, you will see Isaiah 61 fulfilled before your eyes. You will see sons and daughters rise from ashes into beauty, from despair into praise, from wounds into wholeness. You will see a generation marked not by their trauma but by their testimony.

That is the work of the Kingdom. That is the ministry of Jesus. And that is the call He has placed in your hands.

A Commissioning Prayer

Father, I thank You for every son and daughter reading this manual. Thank You that You have called them, anointed them, and entrusted them with the ministry of Jesus. I bless them with courage to step into broken places with hope. I bless them with discernment to know when it is inner healing and when it is deliverance. I bless them with compassion that never runs dry, humility that keeps them dependent, and faith that sees Your Kingdom come.

Lord Jesus, may they always point people to You. May their lives be safe places where Your love is felt, Your truth is heard, and Your presence is known. Holy Spirit, fill them afresh every day. Surround them with angels, guard their families, and let their own hearts remain whole as they minister to others. And may the fruit of their ministry be multitudes of healed, restored, and released sons and daughters who carry Your Kingdom into the earth.

In Jesus' name. Amen.

RESOURCES & APPENDICES

This section is designed to give you practical tools for ministry. These prayers, guides, forms, and references can help you lead sessions with wisdom, safety, and clarity. Use them as a framework, not a formula. Always stay sensitive to the Holy Spirit.

Forgiveness Prayer

"Lord Jesus, I choose to forgive [name] for [what they did]. I release them from my judgment. I give up my right to punish them. I ask You to heal my heart and wash me with Your love. I bless them and release them into Your hands."

Breaking Inner Vows

"Lord, I repent for making the vow [state the vow, e.g., 'I'll never trust anyone']. I break agreement with that vow. I renounce the lie attached to it. Jesus, I ask You to replace it with Your truth: [declare the opposite biblical truth]."

Healing Soul Fragments

"Jesus, I invite You into this memory. I ask You to comfort the part of me that was hurt. I release the protector to go be with You. I ask You to heal and integrate this part back into wholeness. I receive Your peace."

Healing from Sexual Wounds

"Jesus, I bring You the shame, pain, and lies I believed from this abuse. I forgive those who hurt me. I renounce the lie that I am dirty, defiled, or unworthy. I receive Your truth: I am clean, beloved, and restored in Your sight."

Healing Grief

"Lord, I give You my sorrow over [loss]. I choose to weep with You and let You comfort me. I release the pain and the questions I cannot answer. I receive Your promise that joy comes in the morning. Hold me in Your peace."

Session Flow Guide (SOZO Process)

1. Welcome and Prayer

- Invite the Holy Spirit.
   - Establish safety and trust.

2. Identify the Wound

- Ask about the memory or feeling.
   - Clarify the age, emotions, and lies attached.

3. Invite Jesus In

- Ask: "Can you see Jesus? What is He doing?"
  - Ask Him questions about the emotions and lies.

4. Forgiveness

- Lead them to forgive those involved.
  - Help them release and see Jesus bring compassion.

5. Healing Protectors and Fragments

- Ask Jesus if any protectors are present.
  - Lead them to release protectors to Him.
  - Guide the younger part to integrate with the present self.

6. Exchange

- Ask Jesus: "What do they need to give You?"
  - Ask: "What do You want to give them in return?"
  - Have them receive His gift.

7. Closing the Memory

- Seal healing with prayer.
  - Have them see themselves leave the memory with Jesus.

8. Debrief and Blessing

- Remind them of their new identity.
  - Pray blessing over their future.

Intake & Consent Forms

Every inner healing ministry should use clear intake and consent forms. These help create safety and professionalism.

Intake Form Sample Questions:

- Briefly share what brings you to seek ministry.
- Have you experienced previous inner healing or counseling?
- Do you have a safe support system in place?
- Are you currently under medical or professional care?
- What are your goals for this ministry time?

Consent Statement Example:

"I understand that this ministry session is not a substitute for professional counseling or medical care. I consent to prayer ministry and understand that I can pause or stop at any time. I give permission for the ministry team to take notes for the sake of continuity and confidentiality."

Recognition Quick-Cards

Keep simple reference cards to help you identify common situations in ministry.

- Dissociation: Sudden zoning out, multiple voices, memory gaps, "childlike" regressions.
- Ritual Abuse: Extreme fear, coded language, fragmented memories, secrecy around trauma.
- Protectors: Resistant parts, often angry, numb, or controlling. Need invitation to trust Jesus.
- Vows: Phrases like "I'll never..." "I'll always..." "I can't..." that lock identity into lies.

- Common Soul Wounds: Shame, rejection, betrayal, fear, abandonment, abuse.

Scriptures for Wholeness

Anchor people in truth with these passages:

- Identity: Ephesians 1:3–14; 2 Corinthians 5:17; Galatians 2:20.
- Comfort: Psalm 23; Isaiah 43:1–3; Matthew 11:28–30.
- Renewal: Romans 12:2; Philippians 4:6–9; 2 Timothy 1:7.
- Healing: Psalm 147:3; Jeremiah 30:17; 1 Peter 2:24.
- Sonship: Romans 8:14–17; John 1:12; Galatians 4:6–

Recommended Resources

For further study and training, consider exploring:

- Books on trauma-informed ministry.
- Studies on the Spirit, soul, and body connection.
- Resources on dissociation, ritual abuse, and complex trauma.
- Practical guides on forgiveness, grief, and identity in Christ.
- Community discipleship models like house churches and small groups.

(When you release this manual, you can list your other SOZO resources here, such as your Deliverance Minister's Manual, your School of Ministry training manuals, or future books.)

Final Note

These resources are tools, not rules. The greatest resource you have is the Holy Spirit. Stay dependent on Him. Let Him guide every session. Let Him speak through you. Let Him minister directly to the person.

This appendix simply gives you structure. The Spirit gives you power. And together, people encounter Jesus in ways that transform their lives forever.

ABOUT THE AUTHOR

Tom Cornell is the Senior Leader of SOZO Church in Washington state, founder of Walk in the Light International and SOZO Network. Tom is married to his beautiful wife Katy and lives in the Puget Sound area with her and their three kids. He has been in ministry pastoring and teaching the body of Christ since 2008.

He has a passion to see the body of Christ moving from people with an orphan mindset to that of sonship; equipping the body to do the work of Jesus resulting in seeing the Kingdom of God manifested here on earth.

www.ingramcontent.com/pod-product-compliance
Lightning Source LLC
LaVergne TN
LVHW052023080426
835513LV00018B/2118